THE REPUBLIC CHAPTERPLAYS

A Complete Filmography of the Serials Released by Republic Pictures Corporation 1934–1955

by

R. M. HAYES

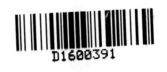

McFarland & Company, Inc., Publishers
Jefferson, North Carolina, and London

The present work is a reprint of the library bound edition
of The Republic Chapterplays, first published in 1991.
McFarland Classics is an imprint of McFarland &
Company, Inc., Publishers, Jefferson, North Carolina, who
also published the original edition.

Frontispiece: *The Crimson Ghost.* The first chapterplay
to be ColorImaged, this is the most grotesque of all
Republic masked and hooded villains.

Library of Congress Cataloguing-in-Publication Data

Hayes, R. M., 1947–
    The Republic chapterplays : a complete filmography of the serials
released by Republic Pictures Corporation, 1934–1955 / by R.M.
Hayes.
      p.   cm.
    Includes index.
    ISBN 0-7864-0934-7 (softcover : 60# alkaline paper) ∞
    1. Motion picture serials — United States — Catalogs. 2. Republic
Pictures Corporation — Catalogs. I. Republic Pictures Corporation.
II. Title.
PN1995.9.S3H38   2000   016.79143'75'0973 — dc20   92-50305

British Library cataloguing data are available

Cover image: Clayton Moore and Linda Stirling beside the title character
of the 1946 chapterplay *The Crimson Ghost (courtesy Photofest).*

Manufactured in the United States of America

McFarland & Company, Inc., Publishers
  Box 611, Jefferson, North Carolina 28640
    www.mcfarlandpub.com

The Republic Chapterplays

McFarland
Classics

This filmography is dedicated with respect and admiration
to the creative forces that shaped and guided the Republic chapterplays:

Franklyn Adreon
Albert Batson
Robert Beche
Hiram S. Brown, Jr.
Ridgeway "Reggie" Callow
Harrison Carter
Taylor Caven
Morgan R. Cox
Ronald Davidson
Albert DeMond
Basil Dickey
Oliver Drake
Jesse Duffy
Lois Eby
Mike J. Frankovich, Sr.
Harry Fraser
Gerald Geraghty
Maurice Geraghty
Norman S. Hall
Arch B. Heath
Alan James
Tracy Knight
William Lively
Sherman Lowe

Edward Lynn
Winston Miller
George Morgan
Grant Nelson
Joseph O'Donnell
William J. O'Sullivan
Ted Parsons
Lynn Perkins
Joseph F. Poland
George F. Plymptom
John Rathmell
Lynn Roberts
Ruth Roman
Barney A. Sarecky
Lester Scott
Barry Shipman
Sol Shor
Sol C. Siegel
Leslie Swabacker
Rex Taylor
R. P. Thompson
Robert G. Walker
J. Laurence Wickland
George Worthing Yates

and especially Nathaniel "Nat" Levine

and to Sylvester "Sylvie" Thomas

Contents

Contents

Introduction

Today the film moniker "chapterplay" is lost in the mists of Hollywood's bygone eras. But just what was a chapterplay and how did they come about in the first place?

One can argue that the chapterplay dates to the beginning of cinema as a paying attraction for the masses. Movies began as one scene shorts, very short shorts as it were. By the early years of the twentieth century they had emerged as multiscene stories with actual plotlines, be they ever so minor, with a beginning, middle and end. What also came from this was the development of certain characters which appeared over and over again in these minimovies. (Chaplin, as the Little Tramp, is the best known today.)

These one, and later two and three, reel films, often released on a weekly basis, more or less followed the adventures, or antics as in the case of comedies which made up the majority of pictures then, of one individual throughout life. While they didn't actually contain a true, continuing storyline, they were series and became so popular that the films were known as the "Chaplin Series," "Keystone Series," "Bronco Billy Series," and such. This public preference for a regular cast in an already established environment led by the middle teens to what became known as chapterplays.

The actual chapterplay differed from the series entry in one major aspect: there was a continuing storyline woven through the entire package. Each episode was itself a story—as with most series television programs—but at the same time part of a whole. In fact a very few series films were later converted, via altering the intertitles and some reediting, into true chapterplays. Also some feature films, which had become common by the teens, were also converted to chapterplay format as late as the end of the silent era. These chapterplays, as they were called in the trade, became

1

known as "serials" to separate them from the series films.* While "serial" became the more common tag, film credits often bore the "chapterplay" notice. For example the crowing rooster (seen but unheard in presound days) mounted on top of the world with the wording A PATHÉ CHAPTER-PLAY opened many an episodic adventure. Indeed well into the forties Columbia Pictures Corporation still billed their serials as A COLUMBIA CHAPTER-PLAY, and on a number of occasions rather more boldly as A COLUMBIA SUPER-CHAPTERPLAY. (They were entitled to their opinion, even if "SUPER" wasn't appropriate in any real way.)

Thus the term chapterplay entered into common, at least within the industry, vocabulary. It was an accurate moniker and if not completely embraced by the public, preferring as they did "serial," it still was recognized by all moviegoers. (Films in general were then known as "photoplays," a tag which hung on in disclaimers and copyrights well into the fifties, but long before passed out of popular usage.)

The popularity of the chapterplay was such that until the late twenties it was almost always considered an adult entertainment. Few prior to the sound era actually featured children in lead roles. Even today the names of Pearl White and Helen Holmes are remembered as stars solely for their serial work, when very few people have actually seen any of their screen exploits. As movies matured, features replaced short subject programs and the chapterplays also underwent a major change. This evolved for two basic reasons. There were so many chapterplays on the market a hook was needed to insure continued interest in further episodes and there were so many thrills offered in features the short chapters each week began to lose their punch. Thus was born the "cliffhanger" ending. Chapterplays now began to feature not just continuing characters and situations but an unresolved, dangerous ending for each episode. The most common on the first few serials to employ this gimmick was the hero or heroine hanging from a ledge, usually a cliff, often a building, hence the new moniker. The trade press latched onto the phrase, then the fan magazines. "Cliff-

---

*Difference in trade terms and general public wordage continues to this day. The most common differences were "talkies" to the public but "talkers" to the industry and MGM to the populace but "Metro" to those within the film community. And there are the abbreviated tags used widely by insiders: DP (director of photography), AC (assistant cameraman), AD (assistant director), UPM (unit production manager) and the like which are not used by the ticket buying patron.

hanger," however, wasn't a tag the public accepted in the same manner as "serial" or "chapterplay" and it wasn't blazoned across screen credits. Rather it was the "vulgar" name most common to the trade press. Still it is used fondly by old-timers and occasionally pops up in writings today.*

By the end of the silent era the movie serial started on its decline, in a sense. This was not the end, rather another meta-morphosis of the industry. The Great Depression, the gradual con-version to sound, beginning in 1927, and the changing attitude of adult audiences affected the serial as it did the entire industry. Previously chapterplays had run with all performances, usually all week. But with money tight, adventure pictures being replaced by "society epics," and the novelty of "talkers," the serial soon became a weekend add-on attraction in second run and smaller cinemas. It would retain its popularity in smaller towns for a few more years, but the major theaters in the large cities had dropped it from their programs for the most part. By 1931 they had totally dropped it. The subject matter also underwent change. Action replaced entirely any "adult" interests in the storylines and children occasionally became leading or at least major support characters, especially in Mascot productions. Even a few animal stars became chapterplay leads. This new "look" in serials made them more interesting to children, and by the mid-thirties they found their comfortable home in most moviehouse programs as matinee and "kiddie show" attractions. (During World War II they would see weekend plays at evening performances in many rural theaters as they often featured war heroics and were still of some value in these areas where audiences retained a fondness for action and adventure films over society

---

*Universal Television briefly had three seriocomedic chapterplays on NBC-TV from 27 February to 22 May 1979 under the umbrella title Cliffhangers. These poorly made "camp" serials were Stop Susan Williams, The Secret Empire (a remake of Mascot's 1935 chapterplay The Phantom Empire, and done partly in sepiatone rather than full color as its companions were) and The Curse of Dracula. The studio foolishly didn't start these off with a first chapter but jumped into each of the stories with "Chapter 4" [sic] or whatever. After 13 terrible episodes the series/serials died. All three were later edited into completely nonsensical features which are stunning in their complete lack of continuity. In the early 1980s a PBS-TV syndicated series entitled Those Saturday Morning Cliffhangers played many outlets. Again the wrong approach was taken, in this instance by condensing every two episodes into one chapter. Rather interestingly all the distinctive Republic sound effects were dubbed over to replace those in the Mascot and Columbia serials telecast in the series. It is clear by that action where the producers of this package developed their fondness for chapterplays. These two pro-grams, and the writings of a few older fans have kept the tag "cliffhanger" alive and in usage far more than it probably ever was in the past.

comedies and melodramas. These cinemas also kept the "B" western alive until the mid-fifties.)

In actuality the stories and characters in the chapterplays had not changed much from the teens. What had changed was the "adult mind" and what was expected from movies during the trying times of the late twenties to mid-thirties during which frame the chapterplay had been reassigned its place in the public's eyes. What seemed so mature in 1915 no longer did by 1930. A heroine tied to a railroad track with a speeding locomotive bearing down on her was no longer the kind of thing many "mature" people felt was proper entertainment for "grown-ups," unless they didn't understand the jazz age and the new sophistication emerging from the "technocratic age" of the late twenties. However, for children they were the perfect form of escapism from all that weighed their lives down. A nickel, often acquired with great difficulty in the Depression era, brought a child great pleasure.

Radio also had much to do with the decline of the chapterplay as adults began a long love of "soap operas" which continues today on television. These replaced action with romance and intrigue, and both were often sorely lacking in the lives of those struggling through the hard years brought on by Wall Street's collapse.

Another factor in the quick decline of adult interest in chapterplays was sound, common everywhere by 1929. The majority of cinemas wanted only "talkers" and any silent film was at a very distinct disadvantage in the marketplace. Serials, being produced cheaply, were the last film type to convert to sound and the first actual full sound-tracked chapterplays did not become available until mid–1930, though several "part-talkers" and musically- and sound effects–synchronized cliffhangers had been available in 1929. Interestingly when the first Universal "talker" chapterplay *The Indians Are Coming,* appeared, though in fact not actually the first "sounded" serial, the trade and popular press gave it tremendous coverage and it was even given evening performance engagements in many cinemas due to the novelty. But it didn't alter the already decided destiny for future episodic releases, regardless of its enormous success with children and adults. (At least part of the success of this serial must be credited to its star, Colonel Tim McCoy, who had been a major action topliner at Metro-Goldwyn-Mayer and who was still riding high on that popularity.)

Chapterplays of the early thirties were provided by only one major studio, Universal Pictures Corporation, one minor firm,

Mascot Pictures Corporation, and a few very low budget producers. In the heyday of the late teens and until the mid-twenties several major studios, especially Pathé, which would become part of the RKO family, had produced serials. Some writers have erroneously claimed Mascot produced nothing but chapterplays, but this is untrue.* The quality of these early thirties serials wasn't good. Even Universal's output showed a cheapness which offended many adults but which didn't lessen the impact on a child's excitement.

When the Republic Studio Organization, nicknamed "The Thrill Factory," evolved from the various minor companies seized by Herbert Yates' Consolidated Film Industries, the movie chapterplay was about to start a new "Golden Age." While the first few serials bore a striking similarity in look, style and pacing to the Mascot items being produced by the former president of that firm, Nat Levine, they had, by 1940, taken on a distinctiveness which became the Republic trademark: fast paced, cheaply made, unmistakable sound effects, excellent miniature and mechanical effects work, spectacular stunt gags, thrilling musical scores, slick photography, fine performances by a stock company of likable actors and actresses, often featuring very strong female leads (a definite plus in the early silent chapterplays), exciting storylines, and a "studio look" which had been missing in both Universal and Mascot, to say nothing of the really low budget suppliers' releases.

Republic literally single-handedly returned "class" to the serial. It was a lower class perhaps, being after all now a product aimed principally for younger audiences, but all the same it was polished, slick and impressive. Columbia Pictures Corporation, before strictly a supplier of features and selected shorts, their most popular being *The Three Stooges* two-reel comedies, began serial production in 1937. But their best shows always seemed far less in production quality than Republic's. In light of the Republic imagery, Universal substantially improved their chapterplays and even the very few indie productions, which would end entirely in 1938, seemed to upgrade as much as they could. The Republic influence carried over into the production of all studios' "B" pictures, but no studio ever managed to equal The Thrill Factory's special effects and stunt work, nor did any facility ever generate more screen quality with such low expenditure.

*Jon Tuska's The Vanishing Legion (McFarland, 1982), is a history of this company.

Republic was controlled with an iron hand by Herbert Yates—known as the "Old Man" and other less pleasant nicknames by his employees—and every penny counted. Since there were so few pennies to begin with—chapterplays for example usually booked out at a flat rate of $5 per episode—no one ever got rich working at the studio, but all can look with pride on what they accomplished there. The company was, after all, a producer of "B" programmers. At least for the most part.

Yates at times attempted to move into the major leagues with, for Republic, large scale productions. These usually proved to be quite successful. The company also owned the Trucolor process developed at Consolidated Film Industries. While never especially good-looking or natural, Trucolor, even after converting from two-color to three-color matrixing formats, and later Eastman monopack base, was color and gave a tremendous boost to many Roy Rogers, Monte Hale and Rex Allen oaters while other studios still turned out "B" westerns in black-and-white, or less often in sepia-tone or Cinecolor (also an inferior two-color matrix system). Sadly the company never employed color on a chapterplay, while Columbia and Universal actually utilized tinting a couple of times. But then the serials never kept the studio operating, they just brought in a few extra dollars. Needless to say Yates' cost control often brought him into conflict with the unions.

Republic was not cheap with their chapterplays. They cost more or less what the average feature from the studio cost, which means they really ran, on a footage basis, about one and a half times to one-third over the cost of a feature. That is cheap, of course, but the serials looked as good as the features, so it wasn't "cheap" quality. Oddly their most and least expensive chapterplays were *Captain America* (1944) at $222,906 ($40,283 over budget) and *The Vigilantes Are Coming* (1936) at $87,655 ($5,039 over budget). What is odd is neither look like they should hold the positions they do. The average chapterplay was in the $140,000 to $180,000 area depending on the period in which they were made. Strangely the World War II years ran the highest. A very few fell under $100,000 and a few cost in excess of $200,000. Serials from Columbia were budgeted in about the same range but looked cheaper. Universal operated in the $175,000 to $250,000 range but they also seemed less expensive. (Despite claims Universal spent in excess of $1,000,000 on *Flash Gordon* in 1936, they in fact made the serial for one-fourth that figure.) Republic's chapterplays normally went a few thousand dollars over budget, but a modest number came in under their planned cost. This fact isn't out of line, however, as very few films actually meet their predetermined expenditure.

Over the years much misinformation has been printed on the actual operations of movies. Writers, unversed in studio management and filmmaking, have followed the wrong courses in assigning credit and fault to films, chapterplays included. I will, hopefully, set the record straight here.

Republic and all the studios, then and now, were factories producing a mass consumption item: films. While this has changed a bit since the late sixties and early seventies when most major Hollywood plants disbanded in-house departments such as sound and special photographic effects, it is still more or less the case. Under this factory situation, units were assembled to provide the needed product. In the case of chapterplays, Republic had a group of personnel who worked specifically on those films. (But as befits a modest sized facility turning out only a few serials each year, these technicians and craftspeople also worked on other projects.) The unit was controlled by a line producer, always screen-billed as "Associate Producer" after the late thirties, who had a team of writers who developed the screenplays. (In the fifties the chapterplay unit was reduced in personnel to one producer and one writer.) The producer and writers created the style of the serials. Once a chapterplay was approved by Yates and his board of directors, it was budgeted by the production department. This department's interests were overseen by the unit manager, who in Republic's case was always a full-time assignee to the serial shooting unit, and the assistant directors, usually two on each film. The art department head assigned the unit art director, sound department head assigned the production mixer, boom operator and recordist; camera assigned the director of photography, operator and assistants, and so on. The casting department selected the players and stunt crew (Republic had six full-time stuntmen on the studio lot) while Johnny Bourke's location staff made all off-studio lot arrangements. Wardrobe came from the studio warehouse or was leased or purchased from Western Costume. With the script complete, the budget allocated, the cast and crew assigned, sets, props and wardrobe ready and locations arranged, the director(s) was brought into the project, perhaps a week, never more than two weeks, before the beginning of principal photography. During his few days of familiarizing himself with script and going over other preproduction planning, the director could make minor suggestions and requests, perhaps asking the camera department for a specific cinematographer or sound for a certain mixer. But these were never the director's decisions, rather they were treated as requests. It was up to the various department heads to make any changes in personnel, all which had to be approved by the studio production manager and cleared through the line producer, who oversaw the entire unit. Likewise on completion of the project the director had no say in the decisions of the editorial, music, sound, sound effects and special effects departments. It is therefore understandable when I say directors working under studio conditions in Hollywood functioned not as creative geniuses, as most writers claim, but rather as on-set traffic cops keeping the shows moving. This is further proven by the fact that directors were given scripts which not only contained the dialogue but every camera angle which he was required to follow. In fairness, however, I will state directors did have some leeway in the staging of fistfights and other action elements, but even these usually were scripted out beforehand and handed to him. Thus the idea that the style and look of Republic's (or any other studio's) chapterplays (or other films) were the results of the efforts of the directors is false. The line producers and writers, in accordance with studio management, created the style, look and sound of the Republic serials (and other films).

Two major factors of Republic's action pictures were indeed developed by directors. While working at Monogram and Mascot, stunt coordinator and second unit director Enos "Yakima" Canutt developed the fistfighting style seen in all Republic films. Indeed this now common technique of having the movement of the fist in relation to the struck (actually missed, of course) body was worked out with John Wayne over a number of films because movie brawls tended to look so fake on screen. At Republic this form of screen fighting became an art as practiced by Canutt, Fred Graham, Tom Steele, David Sharpe, Dale Van Sickel and all the other "gagmen" who worked at The Thrill Factory. The other important bit of action business was created by William Witney after visiting a Busby Berkeley set. Witney noticed Berkeley rehearsed each camera angle of the musical numbers extensively then shot only that angle, then repeated the process for each component of the final sequence. At the time it was standard to simply turn the stunt performers loose and let them go at it while the camera took it all in for a long take. Then various, and always mismatched, close shots would be done. Using Berkeley's technique—which in effect forgets the so-called "master shot" followed by "inserts," is a technique used in many countries to shoot the entire feature instead of the highly wasteful way of English-speaking countries—Witney was able to develop far more exciting, interesting and better-staged fight scenes which didn't suffer from the usually viewed mismatched closer shots. But beyond this one cannot reasonably credit the director(s) with either the success or failure of the final films. Such an attitude is unfair to all concerned.

When the chapterplay came to an end in the mid-fifties, for a few years Republic continued to make features as well as an occasional short subject such as the Vistarama Travel Series produced by Carl Dudley.

What happened to Old Man Yates' miniempire is not difficult to determine. Republic failed to move with the market, and much of that was directly due to Yates' lack of understanding of the changing times. He had allocated money for several "A" features and managed two nicely profitable moves in the forties: he succeeded in keeping John Wayne under contract, in part by allowing him to produce, and with Wayne's help he locked up John Ford and Merian C. Cooper for three features, the enormously successful *Rio Grande* and *The Quiet Man* and, sadly, the failure *The Sun Shines Bright*.

But Yates also made several major errors. He spent far too much money on films starring his wife Vera Ralston who was never a major star despite all of his efforts. (And who, unfairly, has been blamed entirely too much by other writers as a major reason for the collapse of the Republic Studio Organization. She was certainly a better actress than recently published material credits her. And Yates, not she, called the shots regarding the company's output.) He continued to make "B" westerns and gangster features and chapterplays after the market for such had long dried up to the point where profit was impossible. He basically ignored the growing market for sci-fi and horror pictures, except as serial material, which possibly could have saved the studio. As cropped and anamorphic widescreen and stereophonic sound became standard in the industry, he held back, but was eventually forced to give in a bit: the studio began shooting flat pictures for cropping in "VastVision" (including the last four chapterplays) and they purchased the Cinepanoramic (now called Franscope) French-made anamorphic lenses for CinemaScope compatible photography, which he renamed Naturama. However Yates never gave in to Waldon Watson's pleas to adopt stereophonic sound.* The old man considerably increased the number of films on which Trucolor (by this time using Eastman Color format) was employed, but he continued to make westerns which were not so much dead, as dying at the time thanks to television.

Two wise moves were made, though one actually proved to be another nail in the coffin in the long run. The first was the establishment of Hollywood Television Services to distribute Republic films to television. This generated considerable profit, but because it also flooded the market with free "B" westerns, in the long run it literally destroyed the producing arm of Republic Pictures Corporation. The second was a long-term lease of the studio proper to MCA's newly formed Revue Studios, Inc., which was producing TV series for the networks and syndication. Through Revue, more than anything else, the Republic Studio Organization lived actively until 1959. At Republic, Revue made, among others, *The Adventures of Kit Carson, Alfred Hitchcock Presents, Wagon Train, The Restless Gun, Tales of Wells Fargo, Bachelor Father, The Crusader, Fireside Theatre, General Electric Theatre, Heinz Studio 57, Leave It to Beaver, M Squad, The Man Behind the Badge, The Ray Milland Show, The Rosemary Clooney Show, Schlitz Playhouse of Stars, Soldiers of Fortune,* and *Suspicion.* The credits on these series are loaded with familiar Republic craftspeople. For the first time major producers and directors, trying their hand at the small screen, walked through the studio gates: Alfred Hitchcock, John Brahm, Robert Florey, Norman Abbott, and others; crabby John Ford even returned for two episodes. Among the "youngsters" who interned at Republic via Revue: Norman Lear, Robert Altman, Stuart Rosenberg, et al.

But Republic was dying and little could save it. In 1959 MCA purchased Universal City Studios and in the early sixties Universal Pictures Company, Inc. When Revue moved over to Universal, Republic Studio Organization as such was laid to rest. The company still had some theatrical releases, hundreds of titles in television distribution, Glen Glenn Sound, which it had acquired, and the very successful Consolidated Film Industries film lab. But

*Watson had tried in vain to convince Yates to employ a special sound system on Fair Wind to Java (1953). Much later, at Universal, Watson managed to interest executives in his process and won an Oscar for Sensurround as it became known. Universal impressively utilized the technique on several features.

it was out of production. Soon Republic Pictures Corporation became, simply, Republic Corporation. Interestingly many of the department heads at Republic moved to Universal where they became associated with multimillion dollar projects and their names would regularly appear on TV series and feature screen credits. Several, who never dreamed of such at the old studio, would win Oscars at their new home.

Republic sold off its film library to National Telefilm Associates, Inc., and in the early eighties NTA secured the last vestige of Republic: the corporate name and logo. Consolidated Film Industries had already become a separate firm and Glen Glenn Sound had been purchased by Todd-AO Corporation to form Todd-AO/Glen Glenn Studios. As for the actual studio at 4024 North Redford Avenue in North Hollywood, The Thrill Factory, the "little studio in the Valley," it survives today as CBS-Fox Studios and over the years has been home to MTM Enterprises (*Mary Tyler Moore, The Bob Newhart Show, Rhoda,* etc.), Cinema Center Films, CBS-TV and numerous major feature films. For a while it was known as CBS Studio Center (where *Gunsmoke* lived its last years) and for a brief time as CBS-MTM Studios.

The "new" Republic Pictures Corporation (i.e., the "old" NTA) does very well courtesy of its TV and cable distribution of Republic and other properties, its home video library and its own productions including the series *Beauty and the Beast,* the telefeatures *Son of the Morning Star* and *Fire: Trapped on the 37th Floor* and the theatrical release *Cadence,* among others.

As for chapterplays, they did not end with the last Republic production. Columbia produced the last of at least 503 American theatrical serials in 1956, *Blazing the Overland Trail.* The format survived on TV in several series including *Batman, Lost in Space* and *How the West Was Won.* Soap operas continue and they are dramatic chapterplays. Outside the United States, serials continued well into the sixties and possibly even longer, in England and Japan, and probably elsewhere. I understand the Russians have only recently halted their chapterplay output.

As a footnote I should mention 1969's *Captain Celluloid vs. the Film Pirates.* This four-episode homage to Republic — the hero was named Tom Steele — was shot on 16mm and publicly screened a number of times. It was made for collectors and is an extraordinarily high quality production, produced, directed, photographed and edited by Louis A. McMahon and written by Lou, Robert

Miller and Alan G. Barbour from an idea by William K. Everson. Miller was also the associate producer and stunt gaffer. The cast includes Miller (billed under the name Robert Clayton), Doris Burnell, Barbour and his wife Jean, Barney Noto, John Cullen, the late gifted Al Kilgore, Grant Willis, Everson, George Labes, John Kirk, Ken Kipperman, Brian Salisbury, Sam Crowther, Jr., and Art Maddaloni. I can't overrecommend this miniepic. If you ever have the opportunity to screen it, or better yet purchase a print, do so. It is a movie Herbert J. Yates would have proudly made.

*   *   *

Like most males my age, I became familiar with motion picture chapterplays from two sources: television in the early fifties and Saturday morning "kiddie shows" at one of the local cinemas in the mid-fifties. On TV I saw Republic (who were masking under the name Hollywood Television Series because they weren't supposed to be in cahoots with TV), Mascot (who sold off their films and were long out of production) and Universal (fronted by Filmcraft and Motion Pictures for Television, Inc., as they too were in the movie–TV war). But at the theater I only saw Republic releases. Incredibly I did not see a Columbia or independent chapterplay until the late seventies.

While I really enjoyed *Tim Tyler's Luck, Scouts to the Rescue* (a big hit in my house because I was just shy of being old enough to join the Cub Scouts and was eagerly awaiting that event), *Buck Rogers* and the three *Flash Gordon* serials from Universal (or Filmcraft, or whatever name was actually on the credits then), and all the Mascot shows (especially if children were featured, and they often were), my favorites eventually emerged as Republic efforts.

The first two chapterplays I ever saw were *Hawk of the Wilderness* and *Zorro's Fighting Legion* and they are still my favorites though others come mighty close to challenging their lead. By the late fifties Walt Disney Studios had introduced their *Zorro* teleseries and he became a special hero to me and my pals. Due to the great popularity of this character the long gone Lanett Theatre took action that endeared it to our hearts: they ran every Republic *Zorro* chapterplay, except *Zorro's Fighting Legion*, and it seemed they would go on forever. But all things come to an end. The 10:00 A.M. children's matinees and the chapterplays both ceased in 1961, replaced by a triple feature for 25¢ starting at 12:00 P.M. and ending before 5:00 when the regular first run began. Depending on length there would be cartoons, and Three Stooges shorts, but no more chapterplays. (The rowdiness allowed at the 10:00 A.M. screenings was not tolerated for the postnoon shows since the audience was always partly made up of adults. Of course I had already outgrown the "kiddie show" anyway since the average age was ten or eleven. Kind of a moot point since they ceased anyway.)

I did not see another chapterplay until the mid-sixties. Two things occurred simultaneously in the summer of 1966: the nearest TV outlet began rerunning the Universal serials and the new Republic Century 66 package of feature digests from their more popular chapterplays. (The features and serials alternated days.) As luck would have it, I arrived home from work at 4:30 each day just as these programs began and ran for two exciting hours. I saw many old friends from the fifties and early sixties and a few new faces I hadn't viewed before. While at the awkward youth/adult stage I was still able to enjoy these great action tales with only moderate embarrassment. (I was amused by the fact most of my fellow workers, all much older than I, also watched these films for the same reason I did.) My father, who lived nearby and also worked for the same firm although in a different location, was home in time to renew many old acquaintances. He was just old enough to relish with total delight, sans any embarrassment, these youthful fantasies once more.

The year 1966 also brought about another occurrence, or more accurately the beginning of one. I decided to begin a detailed documentation of all the chapterplays, a task which I had no idea at the time was going to be so massive and ultimately difficult. On one fall day in 1966 I started what I hoped would shortly evolve into an enormous, all inclusive, accurate reference source for fanatics of this film genre. The volume you now hold is only part of that data, and my research, begun so many long years ago, still continues today, though with an end much closer in sight. I would like to think this is only the first volume in a possible four piece collection covering in others the chapterplays from Columbia, Universal, Mascot and the indies. All of it has been a labor of love.

Now seems to be the right time for such a reference book on Republic chapterplays. The company has just sold a number of titles to American Movie Classics cable service; two different serial packages are in TV syndication (both running locally), more than

25 percent of all American-made sound chapterplays are now on videocassette with new releases being offered on a regular basis; fans, young and young-at-heart, are discovering or renewing the pleasure of the cliff-hanger; and what I hope is going to be a trend, Republic has ColorImaged *The Crimson Ghost* and *Zombies of the Stratosphere* with spectacular results. Republic Studio Organization was known as The Thrill Factory. This book clearly shows why.

Included herein is every single Republic-released chapterplay, in order of its appearance, with all the credits, chapter titles and casts. The data were culled from screen credits, pressbooks, tradepapers, studio files, Call Bureau Cast Sheets, copyright registrations and any other source I could check. So sit back and once more relive those thrilling days of yesteryear.

The Chapterplays

The Fighting Marines: U.S. Marines Follow the Trail of Adventure

(December 1935)

Credits: *Producer* Nat (Nathaniel) Levine, *Directors* B. Reeves Eason, Joseph Kane, *Screenplay* Barney A. Sarecky, Sherman Lowe, *Story* Wallace MacDonald, Maurice Geraghty, Ray Trampe, *Production supervisor* Barney A. Sarecky, *Production manager* Albert E. Levoy, *Cinematography* William Nobles, Jack Marta, *Musical director* Arthur Kay, *Process cinematography* Ellis J. "Bud" Thackery, *Special effects* Howard Lydecker, Theodore Lydecker, Billy Gilbert, John T. Coyle, *Supervising editor* Joseph H. Lewis, *Editor* Richard Fantl, *Sound effects* Roy Granville, *Sound* Terry Kellum, *Art direction* Mack D'Agostino, Ralph M. DeLacey, *Costumes* Iris Burns, *Optical effects* Consolidated Film Industries. Copyright 16 November 1935 (chapters 1–6) and 28 December 1935 (chapters 7–12) by Mascot Pictures Corporation. Filmed at Studio City. RCA Photophone recording. Chapter 1, 30 minutes; all other chapters, 18 minutes each.

Chapter titles: 1–Human Targets. 2–Isle of Missing Men. 3–The Savage Horde. 4–The Mark of the Tiger Shark. 5–The Gauntlet of Grief. 6–Robber's Roost. 7–Jungle Terrors. 8–Siege of Halfway Island. 9–Death from the Sky. 10–Wheels of Destruction. 11–Behind the Mask. 12–Two Against the Horde.

Cast: *Corporal Larry Lawrence* Grant Withers, *Sergeant Mack McGowan* Adrian Morris, *Frances Schiller* Ann Rutherford, *Colonel Bennett* Robert Warwick, *Sergeant Schiller* George J. Lewis, *Kota/The Tiger Shark* Jason Robards, Sr., *Captain Grayson* Pat O'Malley, *Metcalf* Warner Richmond, *Steinbeck* Frank Reicher, *Douglas* Robert Frazer, *Buchanan* Frank Glendon, *Ivan* Richard Alexander, *Pedro* Donald Reed, *Miller* Tom London, *Gibson* Stanley Blystone, *Red* Milburn Stone, *Captain Holmes* Lieutenant Franklyn Adreon, *Captain Henderson* Billy Arnold, *Captain Drake* Lee Shumway, *Miss Martin* Grace Durkin.

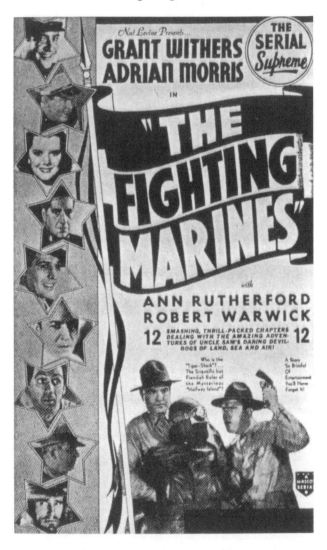

A poster from *The Fighting Marines* (Mascot, 1935).

Note: Produced by Nat Levine's Mascot, the first chapterplay release by Republic came about after Herbert J. Yates' Consolidated Film Industries foreclosed on its debtors — Mascot, Liberty, Monogram, Supreme and Majestic — and established the amalgamated Republic Pictures Corporation operating out of Mack Sennett's Studio City (now CBS-Fox Studios). Nat Levine, formerly president of Mascot, would head the studio's chapterplay department as well as oversee a feature unit specializing—as did the entire organization—in modest budget westerns. The other Republic units—M. H. Hoffman, formerly of Liberty, Trem Carr and Paul Malvern of Monogram, and A. W. Hackel of Supreme—all operated more or less as they had previously for the first year or so of Republic's existence. Their films looked and sounded the same as they had before. The credits were identical with only the Republic name and copyright giving sign that a change had occurred in their creation.

By 1939 the studio organization had become standardized with many of the units once more becoming separate firms, notably Monogram re-emerging as a new studio. Literally all executive positions had changed considerably and all Republic productions had the same look and sound. The Hollywood studio "look" was finally on all films, but the "feel" of the earlier efforts was lost forever. The sheer energy of Republic's first three years of chapterplays was the peak of the motion picture serial despite often crude production values.

Darkest Africa
(15 February 1936)

Credits: *Executive producer* Herbert J. Yates, *Producer* Nat Levine, *Directors* B. Reeves Eason, Joseph Kane, *Screenplay* John Rathmell, Barney A. Sarecky, Ted Parsons, *Story* John Rathmell, Tracy Knight, *Production supervisor* Barney A. Sarecky, *Cinematography* William Nobles, Edgar Lyons, *Musical score* Arthur Kay, Jean Beghon, Heinz Roemheld, Milan Roder, Charles Dunworth, Jean de la Roche, *Chant of the Tiger-Men* B. Reeves Eason, *Musical director* Harry Grey, *Supervising editor* Joseph H. Lewis, *Editor* Richard Fantl, *Sound effects* Roy Granville, *Process cinematography* Ellis J. Thackery, *Special effects* John T. Coyle, Howard Lydecker, Theodore Lydecker, *Sound* Terry Kellum, *Animal supervisor* W. A. "Snake" King, *Production manager* Albert E. Levoy, *Assistant production manager* Herman Schlom, *Art direction* Ernest R. Hickson, *Business manager* Sol C. Siegel, *Assistant to the producer* Leonard Fields, *Casting* Gordon Molson, *Optical effects* Consolidated Film Industries. Produced with the cooperation of Cole Bros.–Clyde Beatty Circus. Copyright 15 February 1935 (all chapters) by Republic Pictures Corporation. RCA High Fidelity recording. Chapter 1, 30 minutes; all other chapters, 18 minutes each.

Chapter titles: 1–Baru, Son of the Jungle. 2–The Tiger-Men's God. 3–Bat-Men of Joba. 4–The Hunter Lions of Joba. 5–Bonga's Courage. 6–Prisoners of the High Priest. 7–Swing for Life. 8–Jaws of the Tiger. 9–When Birdmen Strike. 10–Trial by Thunder-Rods. 11–Jaws of Death. 12–Revolt of the Slaves. 13–Gauntlet of Destruction. 14–The Divine Sacrifice. 15–The Prophecy of Gorn.

Also released as a 7-reel feature version was *Darkest Africa*, in 1936.

A reissue ad of *Darkest Africa* (1936).

Another feature edition, *Batmen of Africa*, running 100 minutes, was released in 1966. The complete chapterplay was reissued as *King of Jungleland.*

Cast: *Clyde Beatty* Clyde Beatty, *Baru Tremaine* Manuel King, *Valerie Tremaine* Elaine Shepard, *Bonga* Naba [Ray "Crash" Corrigan], *Samabi* Ray Bernard [Ray "Crash" Corrigan], *Durkin* Wheeler Oakman, *Gorn* Edward McWade, *Craddock* Edmund Cobb, *Hambone* Ray Turner, *Negus* Donald Reed, *Driscoll* Harrison Greene, *Tomlin* Henry Sylvester, *Nagga* Joseph Boyd, *Tiger-Men Chief* Prince Modupe, *Slave* Joseph Delacruz, *Bat-Man* Edwin Parker.

Note: This was the first chapterplay actually produced under the

Republic Studio Organization and was in fact originally planned as a Mascot production before that firm was consolidated into Republic Pictures Corporation. It was a sequel to the 1934 Mascot chapterplay *The Lost Jungle* (for credits see Appendix). Republic was a bit cheap when it came to retitled reissues. While new press ads and preview trailors were made with the new title, the company would only change the actual screen moniker on the first chapter. All other episodes would still bear the original name.

Undersea Kingdom
(30 May 1936)

Credits: *Executive producer* Herbert J. Yates, *Producer* Nat Levine, *Directors* B. Reeves Eason, Joseph Kane, *Screenplay* John Rathmell, Maurice Geraghty, Oliver Drake, *Story* John Rathmell, Tracy Knight, *Production supervisor* Barney A. Sarecky, *Production manager* Sol C. Siegel, *Cinematography* William Nobles, Edgar Lyons, *Musical score* Arthur Kay, Leon Rosebrook, Meredith Willson, Reginald H. Bassett, Charles Dunworth, Joseph Carl Breil, *Orchestrations* Jacques Aubran, *Musical director* Harry Grey, *Process cinematography* Ellis J. Thackery, *Special effects* John T. Coyle, Howard Lydecker, Theodore Lydecker, *Supervising editor* Joseph H. Lewis, *Editors* Richard Fantl, Helene Turner, *Sound* Terry Kellum, Harry Jones, *Costumes* Robert Ramsey, *Art direction* Ralph Oberg, *Wrangler* Tracy Layne, *Casting* David Warner, *Optical effects* Consolidated Film Industries. Copyright 30 May 1936 (all chapters) by Republic Pictures Corporation. RCA Victor High Fidelity recording. Chapter 1, 31 minutes; all other chapters, 19 minutes each.

Chapter titles: 1–Beneath the Ocean Floor. 2–Undersea City. 3–Arena of Death. 4–Revenge. 5–Prisoners of Atlantis. 6–The Juggernaut Strikes. 7–The Submarine Trap. 8–Into the Metal Tower. 9–Death in the Air. 10–Atlantis Destroyed. 11–Flaming Death. 12–Ascent to the Upperworld.

Released in a 100-minute feature version, *Sharad of Atlantis*, in 1966.

Cast: *Crash Corrigan* Ray "Crash" Corrigan, *Diana Compton* Lois Wilde, *Unga Khan* Monte Blue, *Sharad* William Farnum, *Ditmar* Boothe Howard, *Professor Norton* C. Montague Shaw, *Billy Norton* Lee Van Atta, *Briny Deep* Lester "Smiley" Burnette, *Salty* Frankie Marvin, *Hakur* Creighton [Lon] Chaney [Jr.], *Darius* Lane Chandler, *Lieutenant Andrews* Jack Mulhall, *Joe* John Bradford, *Martos* Ralph Holmes, *Gourck* Ernie Smith, *Captain Clinton* Lloyd Whitlock, *Naval sentry* David Horsley, *Doctor* Kenneth Lawton, *Gasspon* Raymond Hatton, *Magna* Rube Schaeffer, *Molock* John Merton, *Antony* Everett Kibbons, *Zogg* Malcolm McGregor, *Chamber guard* Millard McGowan, *Chamber guard* William Stahl, *Charioteer*

From left, C. Montague Shaw, Lon Chaney, Jr., Ray "Crash" Corrigan and henchmen in *Undersea Kingdom* (1936).

William Yrigoyen, *Guardsman* Edwin Parker, *Guardsman* Al Seymour, *Guardsman* George DeNormand, *Guardsman* Alan Curtis, *Guardsman* Tom Steele, *Guardsman* Wes Warner, *Guardsman* Dan Rowan, *Man* Jack Ingram, *Man* Tracy Layne.

The Vigilantes Are Coming
(2 October 1936)

Credits: *Executive producer* Herbert J. Yates, *Producer* Nat Levine *Directors* Mack V. Wright, Ray Taylor, Sr., *Screenplay* John Rathmell, Maurice Geraghty, Winston Miller, *Story* Maurice Geraghty, Leslie Swabacker, *Production supervisor* J. Laurence Wickland, *Production manager* Sol C. Siegel, *Cinematography* William Nobles, Edgar Lyons, *Musical director* Harry Grey, *Organ music* Raoul Kraushaar, *Process cinematography* Ellis J. Thackery, *Special effects* John T. Coyle, Howard Lydecker, Theodore Lydecker, *Supervising editor* Murray Seldeen, *Editors* Richard Fantl, Helene Turner, *Sound* Terry Kellum, Harry Jones, *Horse trainer* Bud Wofford, *Wrangler* Tracy Layne, *Costumes* Robert Ramsey, *Art direction* Ralph Oberg, *Casting* David Warner, *Optical effects* Consolidated Film Industries. Copyright 2 October 1936 (chapters 1–6) and

From left, Robert Livingston and Fred Kohler, Jr. in *The Vigilantes Are Coming* (1936).

9 November 1936 (chapters 7–12) by Republic Pictures Corporation. RCA Victor High Fidelity recording. Chapter 1, 32 minutes; all other chapters, 18 minutes each.

Chapter titles: 1–The Eagle Strikes. 2–Birth of the Vigilantes. 3–Condemned by Cossacks. 4–Unholy Gold. 5–Treachery Unmasked. 6–A Tryant's Trickery. 7–Wings of Doom. 8–A Treaty with Treason. 9–Arrow's Flight. 10–Prison of Flame. 11–A Race with Death. 12–Fremont Takes Command.

Cast: *Don Loring/The Eagle* Robert Livingston, *Doris Colton* Kay Hughes, *Salvation* Guinn "Big Boy" Williams, *Whipsaw* Raymond Hatton, *Jason Burr* Fred Kohler, Sr., *Ivan Raspinoff* Robert Warwick, *Father Jose* William Farnum, *Boris Petroff* Robert Kortman, *Ranoe Talbot* John Merton, *Captain John C. Fremont* Ray "Crash" Corrigan, *John Colton* Lloyd Ingraham, *Anderson* William Desmond, *Barsoum* Enos "Yakima" Canutt, *Clem Peters* Tracy Layne, *Ivan* Bud Pope, *Pedro* Steve Clemente, *Harris* Bud Osborne, *Robert Loring* John O'Brien, *Senor Loring* Henry Hall, *Dark Feather* Phillip Armenta, *Kramer* Stanley Blystone, *Peon* Joseph Delacruz, *Man* Fred Burns, *Man* Wally West, *Man* Tommy Coats, *Man* Wes Warner, *Man* Kenneth Cooper, *Man* Len Ward, *Man* Frank Ellis, *Man* Jerome Ward, *Man* Sam Garrett, *Man* Al Taylor, *Man* Herman Hack, *Man* John

Slater, *Man* Jack Ingram, *Man* Lloyd Saunders, *Man* Bob Jamison, *Man* Vinegar Roan, *Man* Jack Kinney, *Man* Pascale Perry, *Man* Jack Kirk, *Man* Frankie Marvin.

Note: A fictionalized version of a little known historical situation: American colonists versus Russian colonists in old California.

Robinson Crusoe of Clipper Island
(19 November 1936)

Credits: *Executive producer* Herbert J. Yates, *Producer* Nat Levine, *Directors* Mack V. Wright, Ray Taylor, Sr., *Writers* Morgan Cox, Barry Shipman, Maurice Geraghty, *Associate producer* Sol C. Siegel, *Production supervisor* J. Laurence Wickland, *Cinematography* William Nobles, Edgar Lyons, *Musical director* Harry Grey, *Process cinematography* Ellis J. Thackery, *Special effects* John T. Coyle, Howard Lydecker, Theodore Lydecker, *Supervising editor* Murray Seldeen, *Editors* Helene Turner, William Witney, *Sound* Harry Jones, *Costumes* Robert Ramsey, *Art direction* Ralph Oberg, *Horse trainer* Tracy Layne, *Dog trainer* Carl Spitz, *Casting* David Warner, *Optical effects* Consolidated Film Industries. Copyright 19 November 1936 (chapters 1–6) and 13 January 1937 (chapters 7–14) by Republic Pictures Corporation. RCA Victor High Fidelity recording. Chapter 1, 32 minutes; all other chapters, 17 minutes each.

Chapter titles: 1–The Mysterious Island. 2–Flaming Danger. 3–Fathoms Below. 4–Into the Enemies' Camp. 5–Danger in the Air. 6–The God of the Volcano. 7–Trail's End. 8–The Jaws of the Beast. 9–The Cave of the Winds. 10–Wings of Fury. 11–Agents of Disaster. 12–The Sea Trap. 13–Mutiny. 14–Thunder Mountain.

Released in a 100-minute feature version, *Robinson Crusoe of Mystery Island*, in 1966.

Cast: *Mala* Ray Mala, *Rex [horse]* Zane, *Buck [dog]* Buck, *Princess Melani* Mamo Clark, *Grant Jackson* Herbert Rawlinson, *Hank McGlaurice* William Newell, *Anthony Tupper* John Ward, *Canfield/H. K.* Selmer Jackson, *E. G. Ellsworth* John Dilson, *Porodu* John Piccori, *Draker* George Chesebro, *Wilson* Robert Kortman, *Goebel* George Cleveland, *Lamar* Lloyd Whitlock, *Eppa* Tiny Roebuck, *Larkin* Tracy Layne, *Stevens* Herbert Weber, *Wallace* Jerry Jerome, *Jim Taylor* Allen Connor, *Agent* Evan Thomas, *Agent* Larry Thompson, *Captain* Allan Caven, *Chemist* Ralph McCullough, *Co-pilot/Ed Varne* David Horsley, *Crosby/Harris* Edmund Cobb, *Joe Davis* Edward Cassidy, *Ellis* Bud Osborne, *Fairchild* Henry Sylvester, *Fosdick/Manning* John Mack, *Grover* Harry Strang, *Guard* Oscar Hendrian, *Halfcaste* Val Duran, *Teeker* Frazer Acosta, *Johnson* Loren Riebe, *M-2* Allan Matthews, *Macro* Al Taylor, *Tollar* F. Herrick Herrick, *Mercer* Henry Hale, *Officer* Lester Dorr, *Operator* Eddie Phillips, *Price* Roscoe Gerall, *Radio operator* Anthony Pawley, *Radio*

Ray Mala (center) with angry natives in *Robinson Crusoe of Clipper Island* (1936).

operator Don Brodie, *Radio operator* Buddy Roosevelt, *Rontree* Frank Ellis, *Sergeant* Charles McMurphy, *Sergeant* Jack Stewart, *Spy* Francis Walker, *Man* James Fawcett, *Man* Clarence Morrow, *Man* Loni Ornellas.

Note: It became common at Republic for bit players who doubled as stuntmen to fill more than one minor role in chapterplays and features. In the case of the serials this provides odd continuity when the chapterplay is seen in one sitting or in a feature digest. A henchman killed in one episode would show up later, often dressed the same way, but now sporting a different name. Other oddities also occurred when the same special effects sequence was used more than once. The feature version of *The Masked Marvel*, for example, has the same model car crash in it twice, yet it represents two different incidents. Seen in the manner they were made to be, these quirks were not noticeable.

Dick Tracy
(20 February 1937)

Credits: *Executive producer* Herbert J. Yates, *Producer* Nat Levine, *Directors* Ray Taylor, Sr., Alan James, *Screenplay* Barry Shipman, Winston Miller, *Story* Morgan Cox, George Morgan, *Based on characters created by*

Ralph Byrd in *Dick Tracy* (1937).

Chester Gould, *Associate producer* J. Laurence Wickland, *Cinematography* William Nobles, Edgar Lyons, *Musical score* Alberto Colombo, Jean Beghon, Karl Hajos, Arthur Kay, Hugo Riesinfeld, William Frederick Peters, *Musical director* Harry Grey, *Supervising editor* Murray Seldeen, *Editors* Helene Turner, Edward Todd, William Witney, *Sound* Terry Kellum, Charles L. Lootens, Daniel J. Bloomberg, *Production manager* Allen Wilson, *Art direction* John Victor Mackay, *Construction supervisor* Ralph Oberg, *Set decorations* Morris "Moe" Braun, *Casting* Harold Dodds, *Location manager* John T. Bourke, *Costumes* Robert Ramsey, Elsie Horwitz, *Process cinematography* Ellis J. Thackery, *Special effects* John T. Coyle, Howard Lydecker, Theodore Lydecker, *Makeup supervision* Robert Mark, *Optical effects* Consolidated Film Industries. Copyright 5 March 1937 (chapters 1–6) and 13 May 1937 (chapters 7–15) by Republic Pictures Corporation. RCA Victor High Fidelity recording. Chapter 1, 30 minutes; all other chapters, 19 minutes each.

    Chapter titles: 1–The Spider Strikes. 2–The Bridge of Terror. 3–The Fur Pirates. 4–Death Rides the Sky. 5–Brother Against Brother. 6–Dangerous Waters. 7–The Ghost Town Mystery. 8–Battle in the Clouds. 9–The Stratosphere War. 10–The Gold Ship. 11–Harbor Pursuit. 12–The Trail of the Spider. 13–The Fire Trap. 14–The Devil in White. 15– Brothers United.

    Also released in a 7-reel feature version, *Dick Tracy*, in 1966.

    Cast: *Dick Tracy* Ralph Byrd, *Gwen Andrews* Kay Hughes, *Mike McGurk* Lester "Smiley" Burnette, *Junior* Lee Van Atta, *Moloch* John

Piccori, *Gordon Tracy, after* Carleton Young, *Steve Lockwood* Fred Hamilton, *Clive Anderson* Francis X. Bushman, *Ellery Brewster* John Dilson, *Gordon Tracy, before* Richard Beach, *Clayton* Wedgewood Nowell, *Paterno* Theodore Lorch, *Walter Odette/The Lame One/The Spider* Edwin Stanley, *Cloggerstein/Durston* Harrison Greene, *Tony Martino/Whitney/henchman* Herbert Weber, *Burke/diner henchman/henchman* Buddy Roosevelt, *Korvitch* Byron Foulger, *Oscar* Ed Platt, *Elmer* Lou Fulton, *Andrea* Nicholas Nelson, *Brandon* Bruce Mitchell, *Brock* Sam Flint, *Carter* John Holland, *Clancy* Monte Montague, *Georgetta Clarabelle* Mary Kelley, *Betty Claydon* Ann Ainslee, *Harry/Kraft* Wally West, *Henry Coulter* Forbes Murray, *Joe Crane* Hal Price, *Dock official/Stevens* Leander de Cordova, *Death Valley Johnny* Milburn Morante, *Claude Destino/ Max/Flynn/stunt double for Ralph Byrd* George DeNormand, *Diner henchman/riveter/Peters* Loren Riebe, *Dirigible commander/Crane* Henry Sylvester, *Doctor* John Ward, *Farley* Kit Guard, *Fox* William Stahl, *Governor* Edward J. LeSaint, *Hank/Taylor/riveter/Costain* Al Taylor, *John Henderson* Al Ferguson, *Mrs. Henkin* Jane Keckley, *Intern* I. Stanford Jolley, *James* William Humphrey, *Joe* John Bradford, *Flying Wing pilot* Brooks Benedict, *Secretary/Mills* Jack Gardner, *Teacher* Alice Fleming, *Teacher* Eva Mackenzie, *Bill Moffet* Harry Strang, *Morris* Jack Cheatham, *Patrolman* Jack Stewart, *Noble* John Butler, *Officer* Bob Reeves, *Perry* Lester Dorr, *Pete* Harry Anderson, *Police announcer* Kernan Cripps, *Arthur Potter* Louis Morrell, *Radio operator* Henry Hale, *Clare Renee* André Cheron, *Reporter* Donald Kerr, *Reporter* Jack Ingram, *Reporter* Charley Phillips, *Flying Wing henchman* Roy Barcroft, *Tony* Loren Raker, *Vance* Wilfrid Lucas, *Watchman* Roscoe Gerall, *Whitey* Walter Long, *Wickland* Burr Caruth, *Winch operator* Ray Henderson, *Man* John Mills, *Man* Harold DeGarro, *Man* Henry Guttman, *Man* Edgar Allan, *Man* Buddy Williams, *Man* Philip Mason, *Ralph Byrd's stand-in* Sid Troy.

Note: The last chapterplay produced by Nat Levine who would shortly sell out his Republic interests and move over to Metro-Goldwyn-Mayer Pictures. The first of a quadrology, followed by *Dick Tracy Returns* in 1938, *Dick Tracy's G-Men* in 1939 and *Dick Tracy vs. Crime, Inc.* in 1941. Ralph Byrd later starred in a Tracy feature series at RKO Radio Pictures.

The Painted Stallion
(18 June 1937)

Credits: *Executive producer* Herbert J. Yates, *Producer* J. Laurence Wickland, *Directors* William Witney, Alan James, Ray Taylor, Sr., *Screenplay* Barry Shipman, Winston Miller, *Story* Morgan Cox, Ronald Davidson, *Based on an idea by* Hal G. Evarts, *Cinematography* William Nobles, Edgar Lyons, *Musical director* Raoul Kraushaar, *Song "Wagon Train"* Gene Autry, Lester "Smiley" Burnette, *Special effects* Howard Lydecker, Theodore

From left, Maston Adams and Ray "Crash" Corrigan in *The Painted Stallion* (1937).

Lydecker, *Supervising editor* Murray Seldeen, *Editors* Helene Turner, Edward Todd, *Stunt coordinator* Enos "Yakima" Canutt, *Production manager* Allen Wilson, *Sound* Terry Kellum, Charles L. Lootens, Daniel J. Bloomberg, *Painted Stallion owner* Frank Yrigoyen, *Painted Stallion trainer* Leo Dupee, *Art direction* John Victor Mackay, *Costumes* Robert Ramsey, Elsie Horwitz, *Makeup supervision* Robert Mark, *Location manager* John T. Bourke, *Set decorations* Morris Braun, *Casting* Harold Dodds, *Construction supervisor* Ralph Oberg, *Optical effects* Consolidated Film Industries. Copyright 18 June 1937 (chapter 1–6) and 6 August 1937 (chapters 7–12) by Republic Pictures Corporation. RCA Victor High Fidelity recording. Chapter 1, 28 minutes; all other chapters, 17 minutes each.

    Chapter titles: 1–Trail to Empire. 2–The Rider of the Stallion. 3–The Death Trap. 4–Avalanche. 5–Volley of Death. 6–Thundering Wheels. 7–Trail Treachery. 8–The Whistling Arrow. 9–The Fatal Message. 10–Ambush. 11–Tunnel of Terror. 12–Human Targets.

    Cast: *Clark Stewart* Ray "Crash" Corrigan, *Walter Jamison* Hoot Gibson, *Kit Carson* Sammy McKim, *Alfred Escobedo Dupray* LeRoy Mason, *Davy Crockett* Jack Perrin, *Jim Bowie* Hal Taliaferro, *Zamoro* Duncan Renaldo, *The Rider of the Painted Stallion* Julia Thayer, *Oscar* Ed Platt, *Elmer* Lou Fulton, *Tom* Enos "Yakima" Canutt, *Macklin* Maston Williams, *Joe* Fenton "Duke" Taylor, *Pedro* Loren Riebe, *Juan* George DeNormand, *Governor* Gordon DeMain, *Bull Smith* Charles L. King, *Oldham* Vinegar Roan, *The Painted Stallion* Minister, *Boat officer* Lafayette McKee, *Captain* *of the guard* Frank Leyva, *Clerk* Frankie Marvin, *Harris* Curley Dresden, *Indian chief* Chief John Big Tree, *Jose* Don Orlando, *Marshal* Edward Peil, Sr., *Old timer* Horace Carpenter, *Peters* Lee White, *Rancher* Joseph Yrigoyen, *Secretary* Paul Lopez, *Tanner* Monte Montague, *Topek* Gregg Star Whitespear, *Man* Pascale Perry, *Man* Henry Hale, *Man* Ralph Bucko, *Man* Roy Bucko, *Man* Augie Gomez, *Man* Leo Dupee, *Man* Al Haskell, *Man* Babe DeFreest, *Man* John Padjeon, *Man* Jose Dominguez.

S.O.S. Coast Guard
(10 September 1937)

Credits: *Executive producer* Herbert J. Yates, *Producer* Sol C. Siegel, *Directors* William Witney, Alan James, *Screenplay* Barry Shipman, Franklyn Adreon, Winston Miller, Edward Lynn, *Story* Morgan Cox, Ronald Davidson, Lester Scott, *Cinematography* William Nobles, *Musical director* Raoul Kraushaar, *Production supervisor* Robert Beche, *Production manager* Allen Wilson, *Supervising editor* Murray Seldeen, *Editors* Helene Turner, Edward Todd, *Sound* Terry Kellum, Charles L. Lootens, Daniel J. Bloomberg, *Special effects* Howard Lydecker, Theodore Lydecker, *Costumes* Robert Ramsey, Elsie Horwitz, *Art direction* John Victor Mackay, *Makeup supervision* Robert Mark, *Casting* Harold Dodds, *Set decorations* Morris Braun, *Construction supervisor* Ralph Oberg, *Location manager* John T. Bourke, *Optical effects* Consolidated Film Industries. Copyright 10 September 1937 (chapters 1–6), 21 October 1937 (chapters 7–12) and 16 April 1942 (feature version) by Republic Pictures Corporation. RCA Victor High Fidelity recording. Chapter 1, 30 minutes; all other chapters, 19 minutes each.

Chapter titles: 1–Disaster at Sea. 2–Barrage of Death. 3–The Gas Chamber. 4–The Fatal Shaft. 5–The Mystery Ship. 6–Deadly Cargo. 7–Undersea Terror. 8–The Crash. 9–Wolves at Bay. 10–The Acid Trail. 11–The Sea Battle. 12–The Deadly Circle.

Also released in a 69-minute feature version, *S.O.S. Coast Guard*, on 16 April 1942.

Cast: *Terry Kent* Ralph Byrd, *Boroff* Bela Lugosi, *Jean Norman* Maxine Davis, *Commander Boyle* Herbert Rawlinson, *Thorg* Richard Alexander, *Snapper McGee* Lee Ford, *G. A. Rackerby* John Piccori, *Rabinisi* Lawrence Grant, *Jim Kent* Thomas Carr, *Dodds* Carleton Young, *Dick Norman* Allen Connor, *L. H. Degado* George Chesebro, *Wies* Ranny Weeks, *Captain of Adamic* Joe Mack, *Belden* Herbert Weber, *Attendant* Dick Sheldon, *Black* Robert Walker, Sr., *Blake* Gene Marvey, *Boat henchman* Eddie Phillips, *Boat henchman* Reed Sheffield, *Boat henchman* Frank Wayne, *Boat henchman* Warren Jackson, *Boat henchman* Dick Scott, *Carter* Jack Clifford, *Captain* Jack Daley, *Charlie* Tom Ung, *Citizen* Lee Frederick, *Driver* King Mojave, *Froman* Alexander Leftwich, *Goebel* Roy

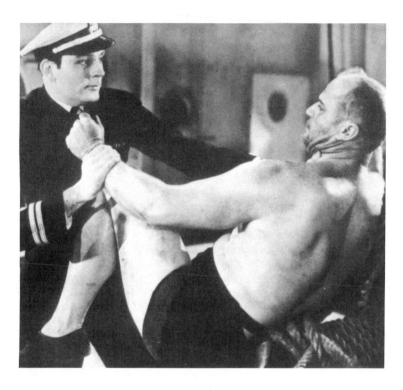

Ralph Byrd, left, and henchman in *S.O.S. Coast Guard* (1937).

Barcroft, *Green* Joseph Girard, *Dock henchman* Curley Dresden, *Dock henchman* Henry Morris, *Dock henchman* Vinegar Roan, *Dock henchman* James Millican, *Intern* Lester Dorr, *Johnson* Edward Cassidy, *Jones* Jack Roberts, *Kelp henchman* Earl Bunn, *Kelp henchman* Kit Guard, *Kelp worker* Frank Ellis, *Krohn* Henry Hale, *Loader* Fenton "Duke" Taylor, *Manager* Harry Strang, *Mate* Charles McMurphy, *Meade* Edwin Mordant, *Moore* Michael Morgan, *Motorcycle henchman* Floyd Criswell, *Operator* Billie Van Every, *Orderly* Rex Lease, *Payne* Alan Gregg, *Pete* Loren Riebe, *Policeman* Frank Fanning, *Policeman* Frank Meredith, *Policeman* John Guston, *Radioman* Pat Mitchell, *Sailor* Henry Otho, *Sam* Jerry Frank, *Scott* Buddy Roosevelt, *Sea henchman* Duke York, *Sea henchman* Forrest Dillon, *Seaman* Jack Ingram, *Slarsen* Dan Wolheim, *Sloan* Roger Williams, *Sniper* Frankie Marvin, *Stationmaster* Robert Dudley, *Supervisor* Audrey Gaye, *Man* Richard Beach, *Man* Enos "Yakima" Canutt, *Man* Teddy Mangean, *Man* Baldy Cook, *Man* Robert J. Wilke, *Man* Leon Davidson, *Man* Jack Long, *Man* Bobbie Koshay, *Man* Jerry Larkin, *Man* Norwood Edwards, *Man* Clarke Jennings.

Zorro Rides Again

(3 December 1937)

Credits: *Executive producer* Herbert J. Yates, *Producer* Sol C. Siegel, *Directors* William Witney, John English, *Writers* Morgan Cox, Ronald Davidson, John Rathmell, Barry Shipman, Franklyn Adreon, Sherman Lowe, *Based on characters created by* Johnston McCulley, *Cinematography* William Nobles, *Musical director* Alberto Colombo, *Title song* Alberto Colombo, Eddie Cherkose, *Song "A Beautiful Shade of Blue"* Walter Hirsch, Lou Handman, *Production supervisor* Robert Beche, *Production manager* Allen Wilson, *Supervising editor* Murray Seldeen, *Editors* Helene Turner, Edward Todd, DeWitt McCann, *Special effects* Howard Lydecker, Theodore Lydecker, *Stunt coordinator* Enos "Yakima" Canutt, *Horse owner* Ralph McCutcheon, *Sound* Charles L. Lootens, Daniel J. Bloomberg, *Art direction* John Victor Mackay, *Costumes* Robert Ramsey, Elsie Horwitz, *Makeup supervision* Robert Mark, *Location manager* John T. Bourke, *Casting* Harold Dodds, *Set decorations* Morris Braun, *Construction supervisor* Ralph Oberg, *Optical effects* Consolidated Film Industries.

Yakima Canutt (doubling John Carroll) and henchman in *Zorro Rides Again* (1937). This sequence was copied and expanded upon in *Raiders of the Lost Ark*.

Copyright 3 December 1937 (chapters 1–6) and 30 December 1937 (chapters 7–12) by Republic Pictures Corporation. RCA Victor High Fidelity recording. Chapter 1, 30 minutes; all other chapters, 19 minutes each.

Chapter titles: 1–Death from the Sky. 2–The Fatal Minute. 3–Juggernaut. 4–Unmasked. 5–Sky Pirates. 6–The Fatal Shot. 7–Burning Embers. 8–Plunge of Peril. 9–Tunnel of Terror. 10–Trapped, 11–Right of Way. 12–Retribution.

Released in a 68-minute feature version, *Zorro Rides Again*, on 16 January 1959.

Cast: *James Vega/Zorro* John Carroll, *Joyce Andrews* Helen Christian, *Philip Andrews* Reed Howes, *Renaldo* Duncan Renaldo, *Brad Dace/El Lobo* Richard Alexander, *J. A. Marsden* Noah Beery, Sr., *Don Manuel Vega* Nigel de Brulier, *Trelliger* Robert Kortman, *Carter* Jack Ingram, *Manning* Roger Williams, *Rurales captain* Tony Martelli, *Rurales captain* Paul Lopez, *Larkin* Edmund Cobb, *Carmelia* Mona Rico, *O'Shea* Tom London, *O'Brien* Harry Strang, *Duncan* Jerry Frank, *Le Rey [horse]* Pair o' Dice, *Jose* George Mari, *Gonzalez* Frank Leyva, *John* Dirk Thane, *Jones* Murdock McQuarrie, *Lerda* Hector Sarno, *Malloy* Lane Chandler, *Old man* Joseph Swickard, *Pedro* Chris Pen Martin, *Pete* Ray Teal, *Raider* Henry Isabell, *Raider* Al Taylor, *Raider* Merrill McCormick, *Raider* Jack Hendricks, *Raider* Loren Riebe, *Raider* Vinegar Roan, *Raider* Forrest Burns, *Raider* Art Felix, *Raider* Fenton "Duke" Taylor, *Starcroft* Brooks Benedict, *Tia* Rosa Turich, *John Carroll's stunt double* Enos "Yakima" Canutt, *Man* Frank Ellis, *Man* Frank McCarroll, *Man* Al Haskell, *Man* Jack Kirk, *Man* Frankie Marvin, *Man* Bob Jamison.

Note: The first of a long running series of chapterplays based on or inspired by the Zorro character. The others were *Zorro's Fighting Legion* in 1939, *Zorro's Black Whip* in 1944, *Son of Zorro* in 1947, *Ghost of Zorro* in 1949, *Don Daredevil Rides Again* in 1951 and *Man with the Steel Whip* in 1954. Some of the later chapterplays utilized extensive stock footage from the previous Zorro tales.

The Lone Ranger
(4 March 1938)

Credits: *Executive producer* Herbert J. Yates, *Producer* Sol C. Siegel, *Directors* William Witney, John English, *Screenplay* Barry Shipman, Franklyn Adreon, Ronald Davidson, Lois Eby, George Worthing Yates, *Based on characters created by* George W. Trendle, Fran Striker, *Cinematography* William Nobles, *Musical director* Alberto Colombo, *Production supervisor* Robert Beche, *Production manager* Allen Wilson, *Unit manager* Mack D'Agostino, *Supervising editor* Murray Seldeen, *Editors* Helene Turner, Edward Todd, *Special effects* Howard Lydecker, Theodore Lydecker, *Costumes* Robert Ramsey, Elsie Horwitz, *Art direction* John

From left, Lee Powell and Chief Thundercloud in *The Lone Ranger* (1938).

Victor Mackay, *Sound* Charles L. Lootens, Daniel J. Bloomberg, *Makeup supervision* Robert Mark, *Set decoration* Morris Braun, *Construction supervisor* Ralph Oberg, *Casting* Harold Dodds, *Location manager* John T. Bourke, *Optical effects* Consolidated Film Industries. Copyright 4 March 1938 (chapters 1–7), 29 April 1938 (chapters 8–15) and 10 April 1940 (feature version) by Republic Pictures Corporation. RCA High Fidelity recording. Chapter 1, 30 minutes; all other chapters, 18 minutes each.

   Chapter titles: 1–Heigh-Yo Silver! 2–Thundering Earth. 3–The Pitfall. 4–Agents of Treachery. 5–The Steaming Cauldron. 6–Red Man's Courage. 7–Wheels of Disaster. 8–Fatal Treasure. 9–The Missing Spur. 10–Flaming Fury. 11–The Silver Bullet. 12–Escape. 13–The Fatal Plunge. 14–Messengers of Doom. 15–The Last of the Rangers.

Released as a 69-minute feature, *Hi-Yo Silver*, on 10 April 1940 with new footage to bridge continuity gaps.

Cast: *Allen King/The Lone Ranger* Lee Powell, *Silver [horse]* Silver Chief, *Tonto* Chief Thundercloud, *Bert Rogers* Herman Brix [Bruce Bennett], *Joan Blanchard* Lynn Roberts, *Mark Smith* Stanley Andrews, *Father McKim* William Farnum, *George Blanchard* George Cleveland, *Bob Stuart* Hal Taliaferro, *Dick Forrest* Lane Chandler, *Jim Clark* George Letz [George Montgomery], *Kester* John Merton, *Sammy* Sammy McKim, *Felton* Tom London, *Black Taggart* Raphael "Ray" Bennett, *Joe Snead* Maston Williams, *President Abraham Lincoln* Frank McGlynn, Sr.*, *Voice characterization of The Lone Ranger* Billy Bletcher, *Blake* Charles Thomas, *Brennan* Allan Cavan, *Brown* Reed Howes, *Joe Cannon* Walter James, *Carpetbagger* Francis Sayles, *Matt Clark* Murdock McQuarrie, *Mrs. Clark* Jane Keckley, *Dark Cloud* Phillip Armenta, *Drake* Theodore Adams, *Guard* Jimmy Hollywood, *Gunman* Jack Kirk, *Gunman* Art Dillard, *Gunman* Millard McGowan, *Gunman* Frank Ellis, *Haskins* Carl Stockdale, *Hobart* Bud Osborne, *Holt* Fred Burns, *Indian woman* Inez Cody, *Jailer* Duke Green, *Marcus Jeffries* Forbes Murray, *Marina* Edna Lawrence, *Morely* Charles L. King, *Morgan* Jack Perrin, *Pedro* Frank Leyva, *Pepito* George Mari, *Perkins* Charles "Slim" Whitaker, *Rance* Edmund Cobb, *Regan* Jack Rockwell, *Running Elk* J. W. Silvermoon Cody, *Sentry* Carl Saxe, *Sentry* George Magrill, *White Feather* Iron Eyes Cody, *Rancher* John Bacca, *Rancher* John Bacon, *Rancher* Griff Barnette, *Rancher* Hank Bell, *Rancher* Leon Bellas, *Rancher* Bill Carrasco, *Rancher* Frank Chrysler, *Rancher* Roy Cline, *Rancher* Tex Cooper, *Rancher* Ed Diaz, *Rancher* Bruce Galbreth, *Rancher* Wendle Gill, *Rancher* Oscar Hancock, *Rancher* Buck Hires, *Rancher* Roy Kennedy, *Rancher* Al Lorenzen, *Rancher* Harry Mack, *Rancher* Frankie Marvin, *Rancher* Lafayette McKee, *Rancher* Henry Olivas, *Rancher* Perry Pratt, *Rancher* Charles Williams, *Rancher* Wally Wilson, *Rancher* Ben Wright, *Trooper* John Brehme, *Trooper* John Bristol, *Trooper* Jerry Brown, *Trooper* Forrest Burns, *Trooper* Enos "Yakima" Canutt, *Trooper* Jack Casey, *Trooper* Kenneth Cooper, *Trooper* Les Cooper, *Trooper* Al Delmar, *Trooper* Curley Dresden, *Trooper* Ray Elliott, *Trooper* Art Felix, *Trooper* Jerry Frank, *Trooper* John Goodwin, *Trooper* Jack Hendricks, *Trooper* Wesley Hooper, *Trooper* Jack Ingram, *Trooper* Henry Isabel, *Trooper* Eddie Jauregui, *Trooper* Chuck Jennings, *Trooper* Glen Johnson, *Trooper* Gunner Johnson, *Trooper* William C. Jones, *Trooper* Robert Kortman, *Trooper* Ralph LeFever, *Trooper* Ike Lewin, *Trooper* Elmer Napier, *Trooper* Post Parks, *Trooper* George Plues, *Trooper* Loren Riebe, *Trooper* Al Rimpau, *Trooper* Vinegar Roan, *Trooper* John Slater, *Trooper* George St. Leon, *Trooper* Burl Tatum, *Trooper* Al Taylor, *Trooper* Fenton "Duke" Taylor, *Trooper* Bobby Thompson, *Trooper* Blackie Whiteford, *Trooper* Shorty Woods, *Trooper* Wilbar Yrigoyen, *Trooper* Joseph Yrigoyen, *Old timer* Raymond Hatton*, *Boy* Dickie Jones*.

Note: Sequel was *The Lone Ranger Rides Again* (1939).

**Appear in feature version but not in chapterplay*

The Fighting Devil Dogs
(9 June 1938)

Credits: *Executive producer* Herbert J. Yates, *Producer* Sol C. Siegel, *Directors* William Witney, John English, *Writers* Barry Shipman, Franklyn Adreon, Ronald Davidson, Sol Shor, *Associate producer* Robert Beche, *Cinematography* William Nobles, *Musical directors* Alberto Colombo, Cy Feuer, *Production manager* Allen Wilson, *Unit manager* Mack D'Agostino, *Supervising editor* Murray Seldeen, *Editors* Helene Turner, Edward Todd, *Special effects* Howard Lydecker, Theodore Lydecker, *Sound* Charles L. Lootens, Daniel J. Bloomberg, *Costumes* Robert Ramsey, *Art direction* John Victor Mackay, *Makeup supervision* Robert Mark, *Set decoration* Morris Braun, *Casting* Harold Dodds, *Construction supervisor* Ralph Oberg, *Location manager* John T. Bourke, *Optical effects* Consolidated Film Industries. Copyright 9 June 1938 (chapters 1–6) and 22 July 1938 (chapters 7–12) by Republic Pictures Corporation. RCA Victor High Fidelity recording. Chapter 1, 30 minutes; all other chapters, 16 minutes each.

Chapter titles: 1–The Lightning Strikes. 2–The Mill of Disaster. 3–The Silent Witness. 4–Cargo of Mystery. 5–Undersea Bandits. 6–The Torpedo of Doom. 7–The Phantom Killer. 8–Tides of Trickery. 9–Attack from the Skies. 10–In the Camp of the Enemy. 11–The Baited Trap. 12–Killer at Bay.

From left, Montague Love, Lee Powell and Bruce Bennett in *The Fighting Devil Dogs* (1938).

Two feature versions were released, *The Fighting Devil Dogs* in 1943 running 7 reels and *The Torpedo of Doom* in 1966 running 100 minutes.

Cast: *Lieutenant Tom Grayson* Lee Powell; *Frank Corby* Herman Brix [Bruce Bennett], *Janet Warfield* Eleanor Stewart, *General White* Montague Love, *Colonel Grayson* Sam Flint, *The Lightning [robed]* Lester Dorr, *Ben Warfield/The Lightning* Hugh Sothern, *Crenshaw* Perry Ivins, *Benson* Forrest Taylor, *Gould* John Picorri, *Johnson* Carleton Young, *Lin Wing* John Davidson, *Sam Hedges* Henry Otho, *Parker* Reed Howes, *Wilson* Tom London, *Ellis* Edmund Cobb, *Macro* Alan Gregg, *Todd* Allan Matthews, *Voice characterization of The Lightning [chapter 1]* Stanley Price, *Voice characterization of The Lightning [all other chapters]* Edwin Stanley, *Ambulance driver* Fred Schaefer, *Bennett* Harry Strang, *Brown* Sherry Hall, *Clerk* Thomas Carr, *Cuttle* Howard Chase, *Dirigible captain* Lloyd Whitlock, *Crewman* Lee Baker, *Dirigible radioman* Jack Ingram, *Gunman* Robert Kortman, *Gunman* Bud Osborne, *Gunman* F. Herrick Herrick, *Henchman* Kenneth Cooper, *Henchman* Jerry Frank, *Henchman* Jack O'Shea, *Henchman* Millard McGowan, *Henchman* Dirk Thane, *Henchman* Theodore Lorch, *Henchman* Al Taylor, *Henchman* Robert Wilbur, *Henchman* Harry Anderson, *Inspector* Jack Daley, *Jacobs* Monte Montague, *Jamison* George Magrill, *King* Larry Steers, *Lake* William Stahl, *Corporal* Bruce Lane, *Marine guard* Lee Frederick, *Marine guard* Buel Bryant, *Marine guard* Tom Steele, *Mikichan* Victor Wong, *Native* Joseph Delacruz, *Newscaster* John Hiestand, *Officer* James Carlisle, *Pawnee captain* Edward Cassidy, *Lieutenant* Buddy Roosevelt, *Pawnee radioman* Wesley Hopper, *Pete* Edward Foster, *Radio operator* Earl Douglas, *Radio operator* Eddie Dew, *Radio operator* Jack Roberts, *Radio operator* Frederick Freeman, *Renault* Francis Sayles, *Room guard* George DeNormand, *Sam* Duke York, *Smith* Ray Hanson, *Snell* Frank Baker, *Soldier* Robert J. Wilke, *Soldier* Joseph Yrigoyen, *Thompson* John Merton, *Watchman* Edward Argyle, *Man* Duke Green, *Man* Ray Henderson, *Man* Edwin Parker.

Dick Tracy Returns
(October 1938)

Credits: *Executive producer* Herbert J. Yates, *Producer* Sol C. Siegel, *Directors* William Witney, John English, *Screenplay* Barry Shipman, Franklyn Adreon, Ronald Davidson, Rex Taylor, Sol Shor, *Story* George Worthing Yates, John Rathmell, *Based on characters created by* Chester Gould, *Associate producer* Robert Beche, *Cinematography* William Nobles, *Second unit and process cinematography* Ellis J. Thackery, *Musical director* Alberto Colombo, *Production manager* Allen Wilson, *Unit manager* Mack D'Agostino, *Supervising editor* Murray Seldeen, *Editors* Helene Turner, Edward Todd, *Special effects* Howard Lydecker, Theodore Lydecker, *Art direction* John Victor Mackay, *Sound* Charles L. Lootens, Daniel J.

Ralph Byrd (with white hat) and henchmen in *Dick Tracy Returns* (1938).

Bloomberg, *Costumes* Robert Ramsey, *Makeup supervision* Robert Mark, *Casting* Harold Dodds, *Location manager* John T. Bourke, *Set decorations* Morris Braun, *Construction supervisor* Ralph Oberg, *Optical effects* Consolidated Film Industries. Copyright 16 September 1938 (chapters 1–8) and 4 November 1938 (chapters 9–15) by Republic Pictures Corporation. RCA Victor High Fidelity recording. Chapter 1, 30 minutes; all other chapters, 17 minutes each.

Chapter titles: 1–The Sky Wreckers. 2–The Runway of Death. 3–Handcuffed to Doom. 4–Four Seconds to Live. 5–Death in the Air. 6–Stolen Secrets. 7–Tower of Death. 8–Cargo of Destruction. 9–The Clock of Doom. 10–High Voltage. 11–The Kidnapped Witness. 12–The Runaway Torpedo. 13–Passengers of Doom. 14–In the Hands of the Enemy. 15–G-Men's Dragnet.

Cast: *Dick Tracy* Ralph Byrd, *Gwen Andrews* Lynn Roberts, *Pa Stark* Charles Middleton, *Junior* Jerry Tucker, *Ron Merton* David Sharpe, *Mike McGurk* Lee Ford, *Steve Lockwood* Michael Kent, *Champ Stark* John Merton, *Trigger Stark* Raphael Bennett, *Dude Stark* Jack Roberts, *Kid Stark* Ned Glass, *Joe Hanner* Edward Foster, *Jimmy "Snub" Madison* Alan Gregg, *Rance* Reed Howes, *Reynolds* Robert Terry, *Hunt* Tom Seidel, *Slasher Stark* Jack Ingram, *Tracy agent* Dick Bitgood, *Tracy agent* Roy Darmour, *Tracy agent* Bob Thom, *Tracy agent* Pat O'Shea, *Tracy agent* Tom Steele, *Gas station attendant* Budd Buster, *Clive Anderson* James Blaine,

Attendant Lynton Brent, *Bill* Maston Williams, *Blackie* Archie Hall, *Brand* Eddie Cherkose, *Buck/sliding henchman* Bill Hunter, *Burke* Douglas Evans, *Burton* Edwin Parker, *Carston* Gordon Hart, *Casey* William Stahl, *Clark* Ralph Bowman, *Clem* Ivan Rayo, *Co-pilot* Eddie Dew, *Crusher henchman* Frank Wayne, *Crusher henchman* Jack Montgomery, *Crusher henchman* Walter Jones, *Crusher henchman* Pat McKee, *Dam watchman* Willard Kent, *Dayton* Sherry Hall, *Dock henchman/fertilizer henchman* Jerry Frank, *Dock henchman* Millard McGowan, *Doctor* Frank Hall Crane, *Draper* Wedgewood Nowell, *Driver* Charles McMurphy, *Duke* Larry Steers, *Fertilizer henchman* Earl Bunn, *Fertilizer henchman* Harry Tenbrook, *Fertilizer henchman* George Magrill, *Parachute stuntman* Bert White, *Forbes* Malcolm Graham, *Foreman* Henry Otho, *Foreman* Bruce Mitchell, *Garage henchman* Allen Pomeroy, *Tracy agent/garage henchman* Duke Green, *Gomez Junction operator* Jack Mack, *Commander Grant* Forrest Taylor, *Dr. Grant* Henry Sylvester, *Guard* Sam Lufkin, *Harmon* Sid Troy, *Hogan* Dan Wolheim, *Irene* Gloria Rich, *Jack* Duke York, *First Jake* Bud Wolfe, *Second Jake* Charles Sherlock, *Joe* Oscar Hendrian, *Jones* Charles Martin, *Carl* Al Taylor, *Knox* Richmond Lynch, *Nicolai Kroner* Harrison Greene, *Kruger* John P. McGowan, *Malloy* Charles McAvoy, *Mason* Frank O'Connor, *Miller* Herbert Weber, *Commissioner* James Carlisle, *Newsboy* Douglas Meins, *Nurse* Jenifer Gray, *Officer* Kernan Cripps, *Perlita operator* Ralph McCullough, *Pete* Charles Sullivan, *Pilot* John Guston, *Plover* Allan Cavan, *Power henchman* Loren Riebe, *Power henchman* Ted Wells, *Power henchman* Buddy Mason, *Proprietor* William Mitchell, *Radio announcer* Jack Egan, *Reporter* Edward Coke, *Rex* Walter Low, *Richard* Pat Gleason, *Sailor* King Mojave, *Sam* Monte Montague, *Sliding henchman* Frank Marlowe, *Sliding henchman* Buel Bryant, *Slim* Frank Hagney, *Snakey* Charley Phillips, *Stanton* Richard Parker, *Stewardess* Virginia Carroll, *Storbach* Frank La Rue, *Sweeney* Warren Jackson, *Max Williams* Harry Anderson, *Terhune* Francis Sayles, *Tire shop owner* Charles Emerson, *L. C. Trendell* Hal Cooke, *Tully* Earl Askam, *Wilson* Brian Burke, *Worthing* John Wade, *Boris Zarkoff* Walter Wills, *Man* Enos "Yakima" Canutt, *Man* Art Dillard, *Man* Wesley Hopper, *Man* Charles Regan.

Hawk of the Wilderness
(16 December 1938)

Credits: *Executive producer* Herbert J. Yates, *Producer* Sol C. Siegel, *Directors* William Witney, John English, *Screenplay* Barry Shipman, Rex Taylor, Norman Hall, *Adaptation* Ridgeway "Reggie" Callow, Sol Shor, *Based on the novel by* William L. Chester, *Associate producer* Robert Besche, *Cinematography* William Nobles, *Musical score* William Lava, *Musical director* Cy Feuer, *Production manager* Allen Wilson, *Unit*

From left, Ray Mala and Bruce Bennett in *Hawk of the Wilderness* (1938).

manager Mack D'Agostino, *Supervising editor* Murray Seldeen, *Editors* Helene Turner, Edward Todd, *Special effects* Howard Lydecker, Theodore Lydecker, *Sound* Charles L. Lootens, Daniel J. Bloomberg, *Art direction* John Victor Mackay, *Costumes* Robert Ramsey, *Makeup supervision* Robert Mark, *Dog owner and trainer* Ger Orvedoh, *Set decoration* Morris Braun, *Casting* Harold Dodds, *Location manager* John T. Bourke, *Construction supervisor* Ralph Oberg, *Optical effects* Consolidated Film Industries. Copyright 16 December 1938 (chapters 1–6) and 28 January 1939 (chapters 7–12) by Republic Pictures Corporation; applied author: Republic Productions, Inc. RCA High Fidelity recording. Chapter 1, 30 minutes; all other chapters, 17 minutes each.

Chapter titles: 1–Mysterious Island. 2–Flaming Death. 3–Tiger Trap. 4–Queen's Ransom. 5–Pendulum of Doom. 6–The Dead Fall. 7–White Man's Magic. 8–Ambushed. 9–Marooned. 10–Camp of Horror. 11–Valley of Skulls. 12–Trail's End.

Released in a 100-minute feature version, *Lost Island of Kioga*, in 1966.

Cast: *Kioga [Lincoln Rand, Jr.]* Herman Brix [Bruce Bennett], *Kias* Ray Mala, *Yellow Weasel* Monte Blue, *Beth Munro* Jill Martin, *Mokuyi* Noble Johnson, *Manuel Solerno* William Royle, *Dr. Edward Munro* Tom Chatterton, *Allen Kendall* George Eldridge, *William Williams* Patrick J. Kelly, *Dirk* Dick Weasel, *George* Fred "Snowflake" Toones, *Tawnee [dog]* Tuffie,

Lincoln Rand, Sr. Lane Chandler, *Helena Rand* Ann Evers, *Red* Earl Askam, *Joe* Jerry Sheldon, *Jansen* Fred Miller, *Dark Feather* Art Felix, *Many Rivers* Frank Hill, *Running Water* Jerry Frank, *Seven Feathers* Henry Wills, *Snow Mountain* Jerome DeNuccio, *Storm Cloud* Iron Eyes Cody, *White Beaver* John Roy, *Bright Star* Joe Garcia, *Dark Cloud* Jimmy Dime, *Geronimo* Tony Urchel, *Indian chief* Phillip Armenta, *Indian medicineman* Chief John Big Tree, *Running Deer* Joe Draper, *Squaw* Gertrude Chorre, *Three Pines* Cy Shindell, *Thunder Rock* L. Y. Maxwell, *White Eagle* Sonny Chorre, *Willow Bush* Wally Rose, *Man* Theodore Mapes, *Man* Jack O'Shea, *Indian warrior* Moe Malulo, *Indian warrior* Jack Minton, *Indian warrior* Charley P. Randolph, *Indian warrior* Art Miles, *Indian warrior* Jim Spencer, *Indian warrior* Alex Montoya, *Indian warrior* Clarence Chorre.

The Lone Ranger Rides Again
(25 February 1939)

Credits: *Executive producer* Herbert J. Yates, *Producer* Robert Beche, *Directors* William Witney, John English, *Screenplay* Barry Shipman, Franklyn Adreon, Ronald Davidson, Sol Shor, *Story* Gerald Geraghty, *Based on characters created by* George W. Trendle, Fran Striker, *Cinematography* William Nobles, Edgar Lyons, *Musical directors* William Lava, Cy Feuer, *Production manager* Allen Wilson, *Unit manager* Mack D'Agostino, *Supervising editor* Murray Seldeen, *Editors* Helene Turner, Edward Todd, *Special effects* Howard Lydecker, Theodore Lydecker, *Sound* Charles L. Lootens, Daniel J. Bloomberg, *Costumes* Robert Ramsey, Adele Palmer, *Art direction* John Victor Mackay, Ralph Oberg, *Makeup supervision* Robert Mark, *Casting* Harold Dodds, *Set decorations* Morris Braun, *Location manager* John T. Bourke, *Optical effects* Consolidated Film Industries. Copyright 25 February 1939 (all chapters) by Republic Pictures Corporation; applied author: Republic Productions, Inc. RCA High Fidelity recording. Chapter 1, 30 minutes; all other chapters, 17 minutes each.

Chapter titles: 1–The Lone Ranger Returns. 2–Masked Victory. 3–The Black Raiders Strike. 4–The Cavern of Doom. 5–Agents of Deceit. 6–The Trap. 7–The Lone Ranger at Bay. 8–Ambush. 9–Wheels of Doom. 10–The Dangerous Captive. 11–Death Below. 12–Blazing Peril. 13–Exposed. 14–Besieged. 15–Frontier Justice.

Cast: *Bill Andrews/The Lone Ranger* Robert Livingston, *Tonto* Chief Thundercloud, *Silver [horse]* Silver Chief, *Juan Vasquez* Duncan Renaldo, *Sue Dolan* Jinx Falkenberg, *Bart Dolan* Ralph Dunn, *Craig Dolan* J. Farrell MacDonald, *Jed Scott* William Gould, *Evans* Rex Lease, *Merritt* Theodore Mapes, *Pa Daniels* Henry Otho, *Hardin* John Beach, *Thorne* Glenn Strange, *Murdock* Stanley Blystone, *Hank* Edwin Parker, *Colt* Al Taylor, *Logan* Carleton Young, *Doc Grover* Ernest S. Adams, *Voice characterization*

A poster of *The Lone Ranger Rides Again* (1939).

of The Lone Ranger Billy Bletcher, *Black* Charles "Slim" Whitaker, *Blackie* Bob Robinson, *Bill* Ralph LeFever, *Cave henchman* Charles Regan, *Cave henchman* Fred Schaefer, *Cave henchman* David Sharpe, *Cave henchman* Art Felix, *Cave henchman* Chick Hannon, *Cooper* Eddie Dean, *Danny Daniels* Bob McClung, *Ma Daniels* Betty Roadman, *Deputy sheriff* Duke R. Lee, *Martin Gibson* Howard Chase, *Johnny* Nelson McDowell, *Jones* Walter Wills, *Sam Lawson* Jack Kirk, *Long* Fred Burns, *Luke* Buddy Mason, *Lynch* Lew Meehan, *Manny* Wheeler Oakman, *Miller* Forrest Taylor, *Joe Parker* Frank Ellis, *Posseman* Herman Hack, *Posseman* William Yrigoyen, *Posseman* Wesley Hopper, *Posseman* Bud Wolfe, *Posseman* Joseph Yrigoyen, *Posseman* Fenton "Duke" Taylor, *Posseman* Forrest Burns, *Posseman* George Burton, *Striker* Tommy Coats, *Holmes* Howard Hickey, *George* Barry Hays, *Cass* Ted Wells, *Rex* Burt Dillard, *Mack* Cecil Kellogg, *Gil* Carl Sepulveda, *Rance* Buddy Messenger, *Safe henchman* Jerome Ward, *Sheriff* Roger Williams, *Slade* Buddy Roosevelt, *Stagecoach driver* Post Parks, *Shotgun guard* Art Dillard, *Townsman* Horace Carpenter, *Townsman* Cactus Mack, *Townsman* Lafayette McKee, *Townsman* Augie Gomez, *Townsman* Charles Hutchison, *Tucker* Monte Montague, *E. B. Tully* Griff Barnette, *Diego Vasquez* Joe Perez.

Daredevils of the Red Circle
(10 June 1939)

Credits: *Executive producer* Herbert J. Yates, *Producer* Robert Beche, *Directors* William Witney, John English, *Writers* Barry Shipman, Franklyn Adreon, Ronald Davidson, Sol Shor, Rex Taylor, *Cinematography* William Nobles, *Musical score* William Lava, *Musical director* Cy Feuer, *Production manager* Allen Wilson, *Unit manager* Mack D'Agostino, *Supervising editor* Murray Seldeen, *Editors* Edward Todd, William Thompson, *Special effects* Howard Lydecker, Theodore Lydecker, *Costumes* Robert Ramsey, Adele Palmer, *Art direction* John Victor Mackay, *Makeup supervision* Robert Mark, *Sound* Charles L. Lootens, Daniel J. Bloomberg, *Dog owner and trainer* Ger Orvedoh, *Construction supervisor* Ralph Oberg, *Set decoration* Morris Braun, *Location manager* John T. Bourke, *Casting* Harold Dodds, *Optical effects* Consolidated Film Industries. Copyright 10 June 1939 (all chapters) by Republic Pictures Corporation; applied author: Republic Productions, Inc. RCA High Fidelity recording. Chapter 1, 30 minutes; all other chapters, 17 minutes each.

Chapter titles: 1–The Monstrous Plot. 2–The Mysterious Island. 3–The Executioner. 4–Sabotage. 5–The Ray of Death. 6–Thirty Seconds to Live. 7–The Flooded Mine. 8–S.O.S. 9–Ladder of Peril. 10–The Infernal Machine. 11–The Red Circle Speaks. 12–Flight to Doom.

From left, Charles Quigley, Miles Mander, Carole Landis, Bruce Bennett and David Sharpe in *Daredevils of the Red Circle* (1939).

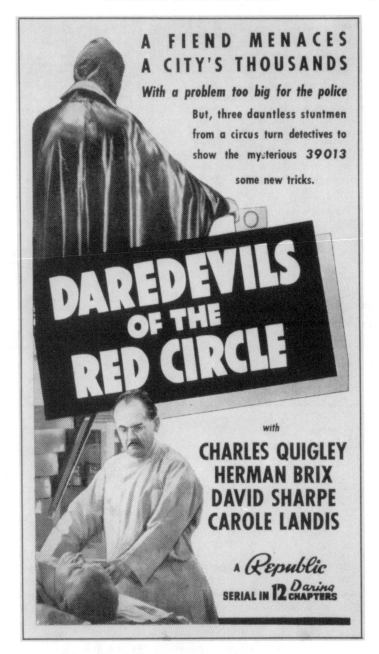

An ad for *Daredevils of the Red Circle* (1939).

Cast: *Gene Townley* Charles Quigley, *Tiny Dawson* Herman Brix [Bruce Bennett], *Burt Knowles* David Sharpe, *Blanche Granville* Carole Landis, *Horace Granville* Miles Mander, *Henry Crowel* Charles Middleton, *Dr. Malcolm C. Montague* Shaw, *Dixon* Ben Taggart, *Chief Landon* William Pagan, *Klein/Stanley* Raymond Bailey, *Snowflake* Fred "Snowflake" Toones, *Sheffield* George Chesebro, *Jeff* Ray Miller, *Sammy Townley* Robert Winkler, *Tuffie [dog]* Tuffie, *First Al* Al Taylor, *Second Al* Bob Robinson, *Nurse Benson* Truda Marson, *Bill* Roy Brent, *Black* Bernard Suss, *Blake* Bert LeBaron, *Bob* Lee Frederick, *Burton* Eddie Cherkose, *Dan* Frank Wayne, *Davis* John Merton, *Derrick henchman* Loren Riebe, *Derrick henchman* Reed Howes, *Dispatcher* Howard Mitchell, *Doctor* Reginald Barlow, *Doctor* Lloyd Whitlock, *Ed* Joe McGuinn, *Foreman* Edmund Cobb, *Frank* Earl Bunn, *G-man* Enos "Yakima" Canutt, *G-man* Fenton "Duke" Taylor, *G-man* Mike Jeffers, *G-man* George DeNormand, *G-man* Robert J. Wilke, *Gas station henchman* Kenneth Terrell, *Graves* Broderick O'Farrell, *Hinkle* Earle Hodgins, *Joe* Jack Chapin, *John* Bud Wolfe, *Kid* Forrest Dillon, *Laboratory henchman* Buel Bryant, *Lutens* Earl Askam, *Mac* Forrest Burns, *Marco* Jerry Jerome, *Miner* Dave Wengren, *Miner* Sailor Vincent, *Newscaster* Norman Nesbitt, *Office henchmen/gas station henchman* Bill Wilkus, *Oil henchman* George Turner, *Oil henchman* Fred Schaefer, *Oil henchman* William Nestel, *Peck* Harry Strang, *First Pete* Edwin Parker, *Second Pete* Walter Merrill, *Police commissioner* Ray Largay, *Power henchman* Joseph Yrigoyen, *Power henchman* Cy Slocum, *Power henchman* Wally West, *Rex* Bud Geary, *Sam* Charles Thomas, *Selden* Stanley Price, *Sloan* Arthur Fowler, *Steve* Jack Kenney, *Substation henchman* Dick Scott, *Substation henchman* Bob Thom, *Substation henchman* Curley Dresden, *Superintendent* Roy Barcroft, *Tank henchman* Max Marx, *Tank henchman* Oscar Hendrian, *Ted* George Plues, *Tom* Monte Montague, *Miner/truck henchman* Jerry Frank, *Ward* Harry Anderson, *Zeke* Edward Foster, *Man* James Fawcett, *Man* Theodore Mapes, *Man* Millard McGowan, *Aerial stuntman* Charles Soderberg.

Dick Tracy's G-Men
(2 September 1939)

Credits: *Executive producer* Herbert J. Yates, *Producer* Robert Beche, *Directors* William Witney, John English, *Screenplay* Barry Shipman, Franklyn Adreon, Rex Taylor, Ronald Davidson, Sol Shor, *Based on characters created by* Chester Gould, *Cinematography* William Nobles, *Musical score* William Lava, *Musical director* Cy Feuer, *Producer manager* Allen Wilson, *Unit manager* Mack D'Agostino, *Supervising editor* Murray Seldeen, *Editors* Edward Todd, William Thompson, Bernard Loftus, *Art direction* John Victor Mackay, *Costumes* Robert Ramsey, Adele Palmer, *Makeup supervision* Robert Mark, *Sound* Charles L. Lootens, Daniel J. Bloomberg,

A reissue poster for *Dick Tracy's G-Men* (1939).

Special effects Howard Lydecker, Theodore Lydecker, *Construction supervisor* Ralph Oberg, *Set decorations* Morris Braun, *Casting* Harold Dodds, *Location manager* John T. Bourke, *Optical effects* Consolidated Film Industries. Copyright 2 September 1939 (chapters 1–5) and 5 September 1939 (chapters 6–11) (chapters 12–15 not registered) by Republic Pictures Corporation; applied author: Republic Productions, Inc. RCA High Fidelity recording. Chapter 1, 30 minutes; all other chapters, 17 minutes each.

Chapter titles: 1–The Master Spy. 2–Captured. 3–The False Signal.

4–The Enemy Strikes. 5–Crack-Up! 6–Sunken Peril. 7–Tracking the Enemy. 8–Chamber of Doom. 9–Flames of Jeopardy. 10–Crackling Fury. 11–Caverns of Peril. 12–Fight in the Sky. 13–The Fatal Ride. 14–Getaway. 15–The Last Stand.

Working title was *Dick Tracy and His G-Men*. Rereleased in 1955.

Cast: *Dick Tracy* Ralph Byrd, *Nickolas Zaroff* Irving Pichel, *Steve Lockwood* Ted Pearson, *Gwen Andrews* Phylis Isley [Jennifer Jones], *Robal* Walter Miller, *Sandoval* George Douglas, *Clive Anderson* Kenneth Harlan, *Scott* Robert Carson, *Foster* Julian Madison, *Dan Murchison* Theodore Mapes, *Bruce* William Stahl, *Wilbur* Robert Wayne, *Tommy* Joe McGuinn, *Ed* Kenneth Terrell, *Warden Stover* Harry Humphrey, *Baron* Harrison Greene, *Judge Stoddard* Lloyd Ingraham, *Doctor* Charles K. French, *Commissioner Burke* Lee Shumway, *Lieutenant Reynolds* Edmund Cobb, *Henchman* Wally West, *Assistant cameraman* Merrill McCormick, *Russell* Broderick O'Farrell, *Dr. Alfred Guttenbach* Reginald Barlow, *First Al* Earl Bunn, *Second Al* Jack Ingram, *Attendant* Ray Johnson, *Barossa* Harry Lang, *Ben/mine henchman* Bud Geary, *Benton* Bob Terry, *Cave henchman/Bill* Bud Wolfe, *Boat henchman* Curley Dresden, *Boat henchman* Charley Phillips, *Bourke* Monte Montague, *Brandon* Charles Hutchinson, *Brody* Charles Sullivan, *Canyon henchman/Jack/Ralph/Ralph Byrd's stunt double* George DeNormand, *Cappy* Budd Buster, *Captain* Edward Cassidy, *Ralph Collins* Jim Cassidy, *Cove henchman* Al Taylor, *Cove henchman/lighthouse henchman* Bert LeBaron, *Cove henchman/hangar henchman* Bill Wilkus, *Crewman* Joseph Yrigoyen, *Crewman* George Allen, *Dam henchman* Charles Regan, *Davis* Bigelow Sayre, *Dispatcher* Russell Collier, *Dock henchman* Edwin Parker, *Dock henchman* Allen Pomeroy, *Dock henchman* Fred Schaefer, *Duffy* Frank Meredith, *Gus Fleming* Jack Raymond, *Ghost town henchman* Eddie Cherkose, *Ghost town henchman* Bill Lally, *Green* Peter Von Ziegler, *Guard* Bruce Mitchell, *First Gus* Robert Hartford, *Second Gus* Kenneth Cooper, *Hangar henchman* Millard McGowan, *House henchman* Cy Slocum, *House henchman* James Fawcett, *House henchman/lighthouse henchman/Irving Pichel's stunt double* Tom Steele, *Intern* Sailor Vincent, *Jake* Jerry Frank, *Jerry* Louis Caits, *Joe* Gilman Shelton, *Johnson* Barry Hays, *Jonas* Ed Brady, *Junior officer* Walter Merrill, *Kranz* Robert Brister, *Lassen* Bernard Suss, *Howard* William Yrigoyen, *Link* Allen Davis, *A. B. Martin* Ray Harper, *President Huenemo Mendoza* Joseph Swickard, *Newscaster* John Locke, *Car 54 patrolman* Milton Frome, *Pete* Ethan Laidlaw, *Price* Edward Peil, Sr., *Forest ranger* Edward Hearn, *Rifkin* Ray Largay, *Shang* Stanley Price, *Lenny Slade* Jack Roberts, *Slim* Reed Howes, *Stanton* Joseph Forte, *Stevens* Forrest Taylor, *Stopes* Charles Murphy, *Telef* Perry Ivins, *Tim* John Moloney, *Track henchman* Bob Jamison, *Trooper* Charles Sherlock, *Trooper* Carey Loftin, *Truck henchman* Alan Gregg, *Truck henchman* William Nestel, *Ward* Jack Kinney, *Warden* Allan Cavan, *Sammy Williams* Sammy McKim, *Gramps Williams* George Cleveland, *Zobar* Tristram Coffin, *Man* George Burton, *Huxley* Frank O'Connor, *Ralph Byrd's stunt double* David Sharpe, *Ralph Byrd's stand-in* Sid Troy.

Zorro's Fighting Legion

(16 December 1939)

Credits: *Executive producer* Herbert J. Yates, *Producer* Hiram S. Brown, Jr., *Directors* William Witney, John English, *Screenplay* Ronald Davidson, Franklyn Adreon, Morgan Cox, Sol Shor, Barney A. Sarecky, *Based on characters created by* Johnston McCulley, *Cinematography* Reggie Lanning, *Musical score* William Lava, *Musical director* Cy Feuer, *Produc-*

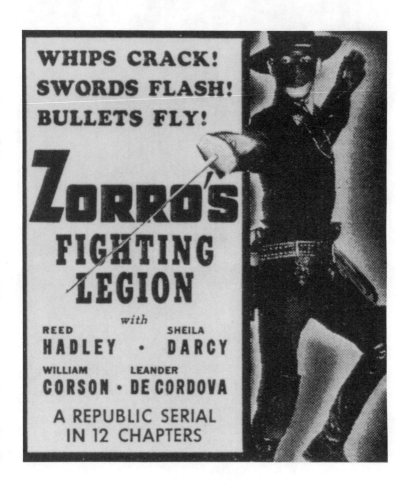

A poster of *Zorro's Fighting Legion* (1939).

tion manager Allen Wilson, *Unit manager* Mack D'Agostino, *Supervising editor* Murray Seldeen, *Editors* Edward Todd, William Thompson, Bernard Loftus, *Sound* Charles L. Lootens, Daniel J. Bloomberg, *Special effects* Howard Lydecker, Theodore Lydecker, *Costumes* Robert Ramsey, Adele Palmer, *Art direction* John Victor Mackay, *Makeup supervision* Robert Mark, *Fencing master* Ralph Faulkner, *Horse owner* Ralph McCutheon, *"We Ride" music* William Lava, *Lyrics* Eddie Cherkose, *Construction supervisor* Ralph Oberg, *Set decorations* Morris Braun, *Casting* Harold Dodds, *Location manager* John T. Bourke, *Optical effects* Consolidated Film Industries. Copyright 16 December 1939 (all chapters) by Republic Pictures Corporation; applied author: Republic Productions, Inc. RCA High Fidelity recording. Chapter 1, 28 minutes; all other chapters, 17 minutes each.

Chapter titles: 1–The Golden God. 2–The Flaming "Z." 3–Descending Doom. 4–The Bridge of Peril. 5–The Decoy. 6–Zorro to the Rescue. 7–The Fugitive. 8–Flowing Death. 9–The Golden Arrow. 10–Mystery Wagon. 11–Face to Face. 12–Unmasked.

Cast: *Don Diego de la Vega/Zorro* Reed Hadley, *Volita* Sheila Darcy, *Ramon* William Corson, *Felipe* Leander de Cordova, *Gonzalez* Edmund Cobb, *Pablo/Don del Oro* C. Montague Shaw, *Manuel* John Merton, *Juan* Budd Buster, *Benito Juarez* Carleton Young, *Don Francisco* Guy D'Ennery, *Kala* Paul Marion, *Tarmac* Joe Molina, *Moreno* James Pierce, *Dona Maria* Helen Mitchel, *Tomas* Curley Dresden, *Valdez* Charles L. King, *Rico* Al Taylor, *Pepito* Charles B. Murphy, *Le Rey [horse]* Pair o' Dice, *Voice characterization of Don del Oro* Billy Bletcher, *Bridge henchman* Joseph Delacruz, *Cantina proprietor* Jason Robards, Sr., *Carlos* Theodore Lorch, *Cave henchman* Jack O'Shea, *Cave henchman* Jerome Ward, *Cave henchman* Millard McGowan, *Indian* Augie Gomez, *Cisco* Cactus Mack, *Dungeon henchman* Bud Geary, *Fernando* Jack Moore, *Garcia* George Plues, *Antonio Gomez* Jack Carrington, *Pistolero* Victor Cox, *Hernandez* Bob Mabesa, *Jailer* John Wallace, *Jaimo* Burt Dillard, *Jose* James Fawcett, *Mabesa* Martin Faust, *Martin* Kenneth Terrell, *Martinez* Wylie Grant, *Orlando* Carl Sepulveda, *Pedro* Eddie Cherkose, *Presidio guard* Max Marx, *Renaldo* Buel Bryant, *Ricardo* Norman Lane, *Rodriquez* Ralph Faulkner, *Salvador* Alan Gregg, *Sebastian* Ernest Sarracino, *Trooper* Enos "Yakima" Canutt, *Trooper* Reed Howes, *Trooper* Barry Hays, *Trooper* Joe McGuinn, *Coachman* William Yrigoyen, *Don del Oro's thorne guard* Jerry Frank, *Miguel Torres* Gordon Clark, *Man* Frank Ellis, *Man* Theodore Mapes, *Man* Henry Wills, *Man* Joseph Yrigoyen.

Opposite: from left, Henchman and Reed Hadley in Zorro's Fighting Legion (1939).

Drums of Fu Manchu
(15 March 1940)

Credits: *Executive producer* Herbert J. Yates, *Producer* Hiram S. Brown, Jr., *Directors* William Witney, John English, *Screenplay* Ronald Davidson, Franklyn Adreon, Morgan R. Cox, Sol Shor, Barney A. Sarecky, Norman S. Hall, R. P. Thompson, Rex Taylor, *Based on characters created by* Sax Rohmer, *Cinematography* William Nobles, *Musical score* Cy Feuer, *Production manager* Allen Wilson, *Unit manager* Mack D'Agostino, *Supervising editor* Murray Seldeen, *Editors* Edward Todd, William Thompson, *Special effects* Howard Lydecker, Theodore Lydecker, *Sound* Charles L. Lootens, Daniel J. Bloomberg, *Costumes* Robert Ramsey, Adele Palmer, *Art direction* John Victor Mackay, *Makeup supervision* Robert Mark, *Construction supervisor* Ralph Oberg, *Set decorations* Morris Braun, *Casting* Robert Webb, *Location manager* John T. Bourke, *Optical effects* Consolidated Film Industries. Copyright 15 March 1940 (all chapters) and 12 October 1943 (feature version) by Republic Pictures Corporation; applied author: Republic Productions, Inc. RCA High Fidelity recording. Chapter 1, 30 minutes; all other chapters, 20 minutes each.

Chapter titles: 1–Fu Manchu Strikes. 2–The Monster. 3–Ransom in the Sky. 4–The Pendulum of Doom. 5–The House of Terror. 6–Death Dials a Number. 7–Vengeance of the Si Fan. 8–Danger Trail. 9–The Crystal of Death. 10–Drums of Death. 11–The Tomb of Ghengis Khan. 12–Fire of Vengeance. 13–The Devil's Tattoo. 14–Satan's Surgeon. 15–Revolt.

Released in a 68-minute feature version, *Drums of Fu Manchu,* on 27 November 1943.

Cast: *Dr. Fu Manchu* Henry Brandon, *Sir Denis Nayland Smith* William Royle, *Allen Parker* Robert Kellard, *Fah Lo Suee* Gloria Franklin, *Dr. Flindens Petrie* Olaf Hytten, *Professor Edward Randolph* Tom Chatterton, *Mary Randolph* Luana Walters, *Sirdar Prahin* Lal Chend Mehra, *Professor James Parker* George Cleveland, *Ezra Howard* John Dilson, *Loki* John Merton, *Anderson* Dwight Frye, *Dr. Humphrey* Wheaton Chambers, *C. W. Crawford* George Pembroke, *Ranah Sang* Guy D'Ennery, *Attendant* Merrill McCormick, *Attendant* Walter Stiritz, *Baggage clerk* Charley Phillips, *Blake* Lowden Adams, *Cardo* John Lester Johnson, *Carlton* Evan Thomas, *Chang* Philip Ahn, *Chieftain* Jamiel Hasson, *Chinese man* James B. Leong, *Corrigan* Lee Shumway, *Dangra* John Bagni, *Fireman* Bert LeBaron, *Miss Frisbie* Ann Baldwin, *Sentry at gate* John Meredith, *High Lhama* Joe de Stefani, *Hillman* William Yrigoyen, *Hindu* Tofik Mickey, *Khandar* Paul Renay, *Koomerow* Francis Walker, *Krantz* John Picorri, *Messenger* Paul Marion, *House boy* Kam Tong, *Richards* Eric Lansdale, *Sergeant* Robert Blair, *Stewardess* Jenifer Gray, *Tartar* Frank Ellis, *Tartar* Henry Wills, *Tartar* Victor Cox, *Russian Tartar* Robert Stevenson, *Telegrapher* George Bruggeman, *Telegrapher* Bill Nind, *Temple guard* Michael Vallon, *Temple guard* Tony Paton, *Priest* Akim Dobrynin, *Tribesman* Carl Sepulveda, *Tribesman*

From left, Henry Brandon and henchman in *Drums of Fu Manchu* (1940).

Jack Montgomery, *Tribesman* Bob Woodward, *Wade* Harry Strang, *Wally Winchester* Norman Nesbitt, *Wilson* John Ward, *Pegai* James Flatley, *Dowlah Rao* Ernest Sarracino, *Dacoit* Budd Buster, *Dacoit* Eddie Karp, *Dacoit* Bob Jamison, *Dacoit* Alan Gregg, *Dacoit* Art Dillard, *Dacoit* Al Taylor, *Dacoit* Jack Roper, *Dacoit* Vinegar Roan, *Dacoit* Bill Wilkus, *Dacoit* Tommy Coats, *Dacoit* Frank Wayne, *Dacoit* Theodore Wells, *Dacoit* Burt Dillard, *Dacoit* Johnny Judd, *Dacoit* James Fawcett, *Dacoit* Augie Gomez, *Dacoit* Duke Green, *Dacoit* George Suzanne, *Dacoit* Fenton "Duke" Taylor, *Dacoit* Kenneth Terrell, *Dacoit* Joseph Yrigoyen, *Man* David Sharpe, *Man* Hector Sarno.

Adventures of Red Ryder
(28 June 1940)

Credits: *Executive producer* Herbert J. Yates, *Producer* Hiram S. Brown, Jr., *Directors* William Witney, John English, *Screenplay* Ronald Davidson, Franklyn Adreon, Sol Shor, Barney A. Sarecky, Norman S. Hall, *Based on characters created by* Stephen Slesinger, Fred Harmon, *Cinematography* William Nobles, *Musical score* Cy Feuer, *Production manager* Allen Wilson, *Unit manager* Mack D'Agostino, *Supervising editor* Murray

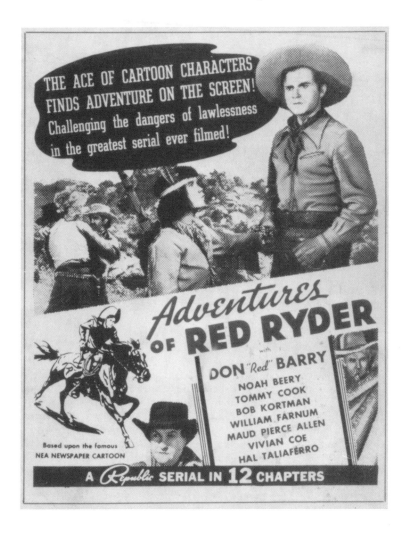

An ad for *Adventures of Red Ryder* (1940).

Seldeen, *Editors* Edward Todd, William Thompson, *Special effects*
Howard Lydecker, Theodore Lydecker, *Sound* Charles L. Lootens, Daniel
J. Bloomberg, *Costumes* Robert Ramsey, Adele Palmer, *Art direction* John
Victor Mackay, *Makeup supervision* Robert Mark, *Construction supervisor*
Ralph Oberg, *Set decorations* Morris Braun, *Casting* Robert Webb, *Location manager* John T. Bourke, *Optical effects* Consolidated Film Industries.
Copyright 28 June 1940 (all chapters) by Republic Pictures Corporation;

applied author: Republic Productions, Inc. RCA High Fidelity recording. Chapter 1, 28 minutes; all other chapters, 17 minutes each.

Chapter titles: 1–Murder on the Santa Fe Trail. 2–Horsemen of Death. 3–Trail's End. 4–Water Rustlers. 5–Avalanche. 6–Hangman's Noose. 7–Framed. 8–Blazing Walls. 9–Records of Doom. 10–One Second to Live. 11–The Devil's Marksman. 12–Frontier Justice.

Cast: *Red Ryder* Donald "Red" Barry, *Ace Hanlon* Noah Beery, Sr., *Little Beaver* Tommy Cook, *One-Eye Chapin* Robert Kortman, *Colonel Tom Ryder* William Farnum, *Duchess* Maude Pierce Allen, *Beth Andrews* Vivian Coe, *Cherokee Sims* Hal Taliaferro, *Calvin Drake* Harry Worth, *Sheriff Dade* Carlton Young, *Shark* Ray Teal, *Deputy Sheriff Lawson* Gene Alsace, *Harrison* Gayne Whitman, *Treadway* Hooper Atchley, *Hale* John Dilson, *Sheriff Luke Andrews* Lloyd Ingraham, *Brown* Charles Hutchison, *H. S. Barnett* Gardner James, *Boswell* Wheaton Chambers, *Len Clark* Lynton Brent, *Bushwacker* Joseph Yrigoyen, *Apache Kid* Joseph Delacruz, *Bartender* James Fawcett, *Bartender* William Nestel, *Pecos Bates* Bud Geary, *Member of the board* James Carlisle, *Breed* Augie Gomez, *Cole* Max Maizman, *Driver* Charles Murphy, *Driver* Eddie Jauregui, *Matt Grimes* Ernest Sarracino, *Gus* Bob Jamison, *Hall* Ray Adams, *Hank* Jack Kirk, *Jackson* Fred Burns, *Janitor* Duke Green, *Joe* Roy Brent, *Johnson* Budd Buster, *Jones* Bob Burns, *Judd* Curley Dresden, *Judge* Chester Conklin, *Judge* Walter James, *Lang* Edward Hearn, *Lem* Jack O'Shea, *Ed Madison* Ed Brady, *Bat Mallory* Gus Shindle, *Masked man* Walter Stiritz, *Masked man* Dan White, *Pete* Matty Roubert, *Seldeen* Post Parks, *Slade* Reed Howes, *Slim* Al Taylor, *Stagecoach henchman* Art Dillard, *Street henchman* Robert J. Wilke, *Trail henchman* William Yrigoyen, *Bart Wade* Kenneth Terrell, *Lon Walker* Charles Thomas, *Water henchman* Chick Hannon, *Water henchman* Barry Hays, *Water henchman* Bill Wilkus, *Water henchman* Frankie Marvin, *Wilson* Jack Rockwell, *Dan Withers* William Benedict, *Ira Withers* Edward Cassidy, *Man* Victor Cox, *Man* Merrill McCormick, *Woman* Rose Plummer, *Man* David Sharpe, *Man* Arthur Mix.

Note: While Republic did not produce another Red Ryder chapterplay they did make a feature series, running 23 titles. Gordon "Wild Bill" Elliott played Ryder in the first 16 with Allan "Rocky" Lane completing the entries. Robert Blake played Little Beaver in all the features. Eagle-Lion later made four color Ryder features.

Zane Grey's King of the Royal Mounted
(20 September 1940)

Credits: *Executive producer* Herbert J. Yates, *Producer* Hiram S. Brown, Jr., *Directors* William Witney, John English, *Screenplay* Franklyn

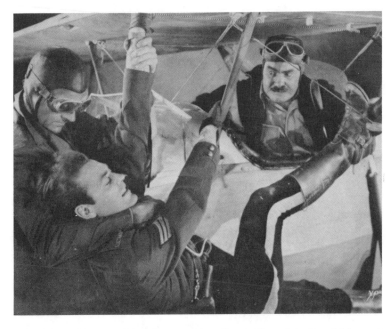

Allan "Rocky" Lane and henchman in *Zane Grey's King of the Royal Mounted* (1940).

Adreon, Sol Shor, Barney A. Sarecky, Norman S. Hall, Joseph F. Poland, *Based on characters created by* Stephen Slesinger, Zane Grey, Romer Grey, *Cinematography* William Nobles, *Musical score* Cy Feuer, *Production manager* Allen Wilson, *Unit manager* Mack D'Agostino, *Supervising editor* Murray Seldeen, *Editors* Edward Todd, William Thompson, *Special effects* Howard Lydecker, Theodore Lydecker, *Sound* Charles L. Lootens, Daniel J. Bloomberg, *Costumes* Robert Ramsey, Adele Palmer, *Makeup supervision* Robert Mark, *Art direction* John Victor Mackay, *Construction supervisor* Ralph Oberg, *Set decorations* Morris Braun, *Casting* Robert Webb, *Location manager* John T. Bourke, Optical effects Consolidated Film Industries. Copyright 20 September 1940 (all chapters) and 30 April 1942 (feature version) by Republic Pictures Corporation; applied author: Republic Productions, Inc. RCA High Fidelity recording. Chapter 1, 28 minutes; all other chapters, 17 minutes each.

Chapter titles: 1–Man Hunt. 2–Winged Death. 3–Boomerang. 4–Devil Doctor. 5–Sabotage. 6–False Ransom. 7–Death Tunes In. 8–Satan's Cauldron. 9–Espionage. 10–Blazing Guns. 11–Master Spy. 12–Code of the Mounted.

Released in a 66-minute feature version, *The Yukon Patrol*, on 30 November 1943.

Cast: *Sergeant Dave King* Allan "Rocky" Lane, *John Kettler* Robert

Strange, *Corporal Tom Merritt, Jr.* Robert Kellard, *Linda Merritt* Lita Conway, *Inspector Ross King* Herbert Rawlinson, *Wade Garson* Harry Cording, *Matt Crandall* Bryant Washburn, *Vinegar Smith* Budd Buster, *Tom Merritt, Sr.* Stanley Andrews, *Dr. Shelton* John Davidson, *Dr. Wall* John Dilson, *Zarnoff* Paul McVey, *Admiral Johnson* Lucien Prival, *Captain Tarner* Norman Willis, *Le Couteau* Tony Paton, *Al* Kenneth Terrell, *Bayliss* Charles Thomas, *Bill* Bill Wilkus, *Blake* Theodore Mapes, *Harold Bolton* Major Sam Harris, *Brakeman* George Plues, *Brant* Frank Wayne, *Carter* Richard Simmons, *Dinwoodie* Loren Riebe, *Doyle* Wallace Reid, Jr., *Hallett* William Justice, *Bob Hastings* William Stahl, *Higgins* John Bagni, *Joe* Earl Bunn, *Kelly* Curley Dresden, *Klondike* Bud Geary, *Knifefighter* Dave Marks, *Lieutenant* Robert Wayne, *MacCloud* William Kellogg, *Mike* Tommy Coats, *Mills* Alan Gregg, *Cripple* Denny Sullivan, *Cripple* Walter Low, *Cripple* George Ford, *Pete* Bob Jamison, *Radioman* Dale Van Sickel, *Red* Al Taylor, *Sanitarium henchman* Cy Slocum, *Sergeant* Douglas Evans, *Smelter henchman* Fenton "Duke" Taylor, *Smelter henchman* James Fawcett, *Man* Duke Green, *Man* David Sharpe, *Man* George DeNormand.

Note: Sequel was *King of the Mounties* (1942) followed by two other Mountie chapterplays, *Dangers of the Canadian Mounted* (1948) and *Canadian Mounties vs. Atomic Invaders* (1953).

Mysterious Doctor Satan
(13 December 1940)

Credits: *Executive producer* Herbert J. Yates, *Producer* Hiram S. Brown, Jr., *Directors* William Witney, John English, *Writers* Franklyn Adreon, Ronald Davidson, Norman S. Hall, Joseph F. Poland, Barney A. Sarecky, Sol Shor, *Cinematography* William Nobles, *Musical score* Cy Feuer, *Production manager* Allen Wilson, *Unit manager* Mack D'Agostino, *Editors* Edward Todd, William Thompson, *Special effects* Howard Lydecker, Theodore Lydecker, *Sound* Charles L. Lootens, Daniel J. Bloomberg, *Costumes* Robert Ramsey, Adele Palmer, *Makeup supervision* Robert Mark, *Art direction* John Victor Mackay, *Construction supervisor* Ralph Oberg, *Set decorations* Morris Braun, *Casting* Robert Webb, *Location manager* John T. Bourke, *Optical effects* Consolidated Film Industries. Copyright 13 December 1940 (all chapters) by Republic Pictures Corporation; applied author: Republic Productions, Inc. RCA Photophone recording. Chapter 1, 31 minutes; all other chapters, 17 minutes each.

Chapter titles: 1-Return of the Copperhead. 2-Thirteen Steps. 3-Undersea Tomb. 4-The Human Bomb. 5-Doctor Satan's Man of Steel. 6-Double Cross. 7-The Monster Strikes. 8-Highway of Death. 9-Double Jeopardy. 10-Bridge of Peril. 11-Death Closes In. 12-Crack-Up. 13-Disguised. 14-The Flaming Coffin. 15-Doctor Satan Strikes.

From left, Eduardo Cianelli and Robert Wilcox in *Mysterious Doctor Satan* (1940).

Released in a 100-minute feature version, *Doctor Satan's Robot*, in 1966.

Cast: *Doctor Satan* Eduardo Cianelli, *Bob Wayne/The Copperhead* Robert Wilcox, *Speed Martin* William Newell, *Professor Thomas Scott* C. Montague Shaw, *Lois Scott* Ella Neal, *Alice Brent* Dorothy Herbert, *Governor Bronson* Charles Trowbridge, *Chief of Police Rand* Jack Mulhall, *Colonel Bevans* Edwin Stanley, *Stoner* Walter McGrail, *Gort* Joe McGuinn, *Hallett* Bud Geary, *Corbay* Paul Marion, *Ross* Archie Twitchell, *Scarlett* Lynton Brent, *Corwin* Kenneth Terrell, *Joe* Al Taylor, *Red* Alan Gregg, *Al* James Fawcett, *Barton* Edward Cassidy, *Brock* William Stahl, *Burns* Frank Conklan, Sr., *Chuck* Edwin Parker, *Co-pilot* James Bush, *Davis* Harry Strang, *Duke* Duke Green, *Fallon* Bert LeBaron, *Gas station attendant* Eddie Dew, *Glover* Ted Stanhope, *Gray* John Bagni, *Green* Jerry Jerome, *House henchman* Jack O'Shea, *Jake* Al Seymour, *Lathrop* Kenneth Harlan, *Mike* Ernest Sarracino, *Nurse* Virginia Carroll, *Officer* Fred Criswell, *Palmer* Wally West, *Panamint Pete* Frank Brownlee, *Perry* Robert Wayne, *Plant henchman* Frank Ellis, *Plant henchman* Patrick Kelly, *Proprietor* Charles Hutchison, *Sailor* Enos "Yakima" Canutt, *Sailor* Bud Wolfe, *Smith* Hal Price, *Spike* George Allen, *Steve* Marten Lamont, *Truck henchman* Tom Steele, *Truck henchman* Bill Wilkus, *Wagner* Davison Clark, *Watkins* Fenton "Duke" Taylor, *Wells* Tristram Coffin, *Williams* Lloyd Whitlock, *Man* Sam Garrett, *Man* Bob Rogers, *Man* Cy Slocum, *Man* Fred Schaefer, *Man* David Sharpe, *Man* William Yrigoyen, *Woman* Helen Thurston.

Adventures of Captain Marvel
(28 March 1941)

Credits: *Executive producer* Herbert J. Yates, *Producer* Hiram S. Brown, Jr., *Directors* William Witney, John English, *Screenplay* Sol Shor, Ronald Davidson, Norman S. Hall, Joseph F. Poland, Arch B. Heath, *Based on characters created by* William Parker, Charles Clarence Beck, *Cinematography* William Nobles, *Process cinematography* Ellis J. Thackery, *Musical score* Cy Feuer, Mort Glickman, William Lava, Ross Di Maggio, *Musical director* Cy Feuer, *Production manager* Allen Wilson, *Unit manager* Mack D'Agostino, *Assistant directors* Louis Germanprez, R. G. Springsteen, *Special effects* Howard Lydecker, Theodore Lydecker, *Costumes* Robert Ramsey, Adele Palmer, *Makeup supervision* Robert Mark, *Art direction* John Victor Mackay, *Supervising editor* Murray Seldeen, *Editors* Edward Todd, William Thompson, *Sound* Charles L. Lootens, Daniel J. Bloomberg, *Location manager* John T. Bourke, *Set decorations* Morris Braun, *Construction supervisor* Ralph Oberg, *Casting* Robert Webb, *Optical effects* Consolidated Film Industries. Copyright 28 March 1941 (all chapters) by Republic Pictures Corporation; applied author: Republic Productions, Inc. RCA Photophone recording. Chapter 1, 30 minutes; all other chapters, 17 minutes each.

Chapter titles: 1–Curse of the Scorpion. 2–The Guillotine. 3–Time Bomb. 4–Death Takes the Wheel. 5–The Scorpion Strikes. 6–Lens of Death. 7–Human Targets. 8–Boomerang. 9–Dead Man's Trap. 10–Doom Ship. 11–Valley of Death. 12–Captain Marvel's Secret.

Rereleased as *Return of Captain Marvel.* A 6-reel feature version was released outside the United States but never exhibited domestically.

Cast: *Captain Marvel* Tom Tyler, *Billy Batson* Frank Coghlan, Jr., *Whitey Murphy* William Benedict, *Betty Wallace* Louise Currie, *Professor Luther Bentley/The Scorpion* Harry Worth, *John Malcolm* Robert Strange, *Henry Carlyle* Bryant Washburn, *Tal Chotali* John Davidson, *Dr. Stephen Lang* George Pembroke, *Dwight Fisher* Peter George Lynn, *Rahman Bar* Reed Hadley, *James Howell* Jack Mulhall, *Barnett* Kenneth Duncan, *Shazam* Nigel de Brulier, *Cowan* John Bagni, *Martin* Carleton Young, *Major Rawley* Leland Hodgson, *Owens* Stanley Price, *Akbar* Ernest Sarracino, *Chan Lai* Tetsu Komai, *Voice characterization of The Scorpion* Gerald Mohr, *Ali* Paul Lopez, *Laboratory henchman/curio henchman* Loren Riebe, *Laboratory henchman* Fenton "Duke" Taylor, *Curio henchman* James Fawcett, *Colonel Hudson* Major Sam Harris, *Captain Dodge* Edward Cassidy, *Benson* Wilson Benge, *Brandon* Jerry Jerome, *Bridge henchman* Richard Crockett, *Carlson* Chuck Morrison, *Carter* Francis Sayles, *Lieutenant* Eddie Dew, *Dam henchman* Earl Bunn, *Dam henchman* George Suzanne, *Seaman* Theodore Mapes, *Gus* Frank Marlowe, *Hamil* Armand Cortes, *Hawks* Kenneth Terrell, *Lefty* Lynton Brent, *Native chief* Al Kikume, *Native* Augie Gomez, *Native* Al Taylor, *Native* Curley

A reissue ad for *Adventures of Captain Marvel* (1966).

Dresden, *Native* Henry Wills, *Native* Steve Clemente, *Pete* Bud Geary, *Radio sergeant* Martin Lamont, *Sentry* Carl Zwolsman, *Steve* Frank Wayne, *Trucker* Ray Hanson, *Man* Victor Cox, *Man* Joseph Delacruz, *Tom Tyler's stunt double* David Sharpe.

Edgar Rice Burroughs' Jungle Girl
(21 June 1941)

Credits: *Executive producer* Herbert J. Yates, *Producer* Hiram S. Brown, Jr., *Directors* William Witney, John English, *Screenplay* Ronald Davidson, Norman S. Hall, William Lively, Joseph O'Donnell, Joseph F. Poland, Alfred Batson, *Based on the novel "Jungle Girl"* by Edgar Rice Burroughs, *Cinematography* Reggie Lanning, *Musical score* Cy Feuer, *Production manager* Allen Wilson, *Unit manager* Mack D'Agostino, *Supervising editor* Murray Seldeen, *Editors* Edward Todd, William Thompson, *Special effects* Howard Lydecker, Theodore Lydecker, *Sound* Charles L. Lootens, Daniel J. Bloomberg, *Costumes* Robert Ramsey, Adele Palmer, *Makeup supervision* Robert Mark, *Art direction* John Victor Mackay, *Casting* Robert Webb, *Location manager* John T. Bourke, *Construction supervisor* Ralph Oberg, *Set decorations* Morris Braun, *Optical effects* Consolidated Film Industries. Copyright 21 June 1941 (all chapters) by Republic Pictures Corporation; applied author: Republic Productions, Inc. RCA photophone recording. Chapter 1, 29 minutes; all other chapters, 17 minutes each.

Chapter titles: 1–Death of Voodoo. 2–Queen of Beasts. 3–River of

From left, Frances Gifford, Frank Lackteen in *Edgar Rice Burroughs' Jungle Girl* (1941).

Fire. 4–Treachery. 5–Jungle Vengeance. 6–Tribal Fury. 7–The Poison
Dart. 8–Man Trap. 9–Treasure Tomb. 10–Jungle Killer. 11–Dangerous
Secret. 12–Trapped. 13–Ambush. 14–Diamond Trail. 15–Flight to Free-
dom.

Rereleased in 1947.

Cast: *Nyoka Meredith* Frances Gifford, *Jack Stanton* Tom Neal, *John
Meredith/Bradley Meredith* Trevor Bardette, *Slick Latimer* Gerald Mohr,
Curly Rogers Eddie Acuff, *Shamba* Frank Lackteen, *Wakimbu* Tommy
Cook, *Bombo* Robert Barron, *Lutembi* Al Kikume, *Brock* Bud Geary, *Clag-
gett* Al Taylor, *Ted Bone* Joe McGuinn, *Lion chief* Jerry Frank, *Mananga*
Kenneth Terrell, *Man* Enos "Yakima" Canutt, *Man* Duke Green, *Man*
David Sharpe, *Man* Harry Smith, *Man* Tom Steele, *Man* Fenton "Duke"
Taylor, *Frances Gifford's stunt double* Helen Thurston.

Note: Sequel was *Perils of Nyoka* (1942) followed by two pseudo-
sequels *The Tiger Woman* (1944) and *Panther Girl of the Kongo* (1955).

King of the Texas Rangers
(4 October 1941)

Credits: *Executive producer* Herbert J. Yates, *Producer* Hiram S.
Brown, Jr., *Directors* William Witney, John English, *Writers* Ronald David-
son, Norman S. Hall, Joseph F. Poland, William Lively, Joseph O'Donnell,
Cinematography Reggie Lanning, *Musical score* Cy Feuer, *Orchestrations*
Mort Glickman, Darrell Calker, Leo Erdody, *Production manager* Allen
Wilson, *Unit manager* Mack D'Agostino, *Supervising editor* Murray Sel-
deen, *Editors* William Thompson, Edward Todd, *Special effects* Howard
Lydecker, Theodore Lydecker, *Sound* Charles L. Lootens, Daniel J.
Bloomberg, *Costumes* Robert Ramsey, Adele Palmer, *Makeup supervision*
Robert Mark, *Art direction* John Victor Mackay, *Set decorations* Morris
Braun, *Construction supervisor* Ralph Oberg, *Casting* Robert Webb, *Loca-
tion manager* John T. Bourke, *Optical effects* Consolidated Film Industries.
Copyright 2 October 1941 (all chapters) by Republic Pictures Corporation;
applied author: Republic Productions, Inc. RCA Photophone recording.
Chapter 1, 30 minutes; all other chapters, 17 minutes each.

Chapter titles: 1–The Fifth Column Strikes. 2–Dead End. 3–Man
Hunt. 4–Trapped. 5–Test Flight. 6–Double Danger. 7–Death Takes the
Witness. 8–Counterfeit Trail. 9–Ambush. 10–Sky Raiders. 11–Trail of
Death. 12–Code of the Rangers.

Cast: *Sergeant Tom J. King, Jr.* Slingin' Sammy Baugh, *John Barton*
Neil Hamilton, *Sally Crane* Pauline Moore, *Pedro Garcia* Duncan
Renaldo, *Robert Crawford* Charles Trowbridge, *Colonel Lee Avery* Herbert
Rawlinson, *Pop Evans* Frank Darien, *His Excellency* Robert O. Davis, *Cap-
tain Tom J. King, Sr.* Monte Blue, *A. J. Lynch* Stanley Blystone, *Wichita
Bates* Kermit Maynard, *Ross* Roy Barcroft, *Nick* Kenneth Duncan, *Shorty*

From left, Slingin' Sammy Baugh and Duncan Renaldo in *King of the Texas Rangers* (1941).

Jack Ingram, *Blake* Robert Barron, *Cole* Frank Bruno, *Dade* Monte Montague, *Professor Nelson* Joseph Forte, *Captain* Lucien Prival, *Army observer* Paul Gustine, *L. H. Bowen* Henry Hall, *Hank Breen* William Kellogg, *Red Cameron* Richard Simmons, *Carl* Alan Gregg, *Carlos* Iron Eyes Cody, *Clerk* Forrest Taylor, *Coach* Lee Shumway, *Cowan* Ernest Sarracino, *Cramer* Bud Geary, *Dam guard* Bob Jamison, *Dave* John Jamison, *Derrick henchman* Dick Scott, *Derrick henchman* Bud Wolfe, *Dirigible henchman* Barry Hays, *Dirigible henchman* Earl Bunn, *Lieutenant* George Barrows, *Lieutenant* Pat O'Shea, *Dock henchman* Bert LeBaron, *Ed* Jerry Jerome, *Eduardo* Bobby Barker, *Gate guard* Forrest Burns, *Gus* Max Maizman, *Jake* Charles "Slim" Whitaker, *Stub Latner* Jack Chapin, *Johnny Logan* Howard Hughes, *Ronnie Nelson* Michael Owen, *Oil field henchman* Kenneth Terrell, *Porter* Hooper Atchley, *Radio operator* Otto Reichow, *Raider* Chick Hannon, *Raider* Herman Hack, *Rancho henchman* Tommy Coats, *Rancho henchman* Charles Thomas, *Rancho henchman* Bob Robinson, *Rancho henchman* Carlie Taylor, *Sedley* Edward Cassidy, *Sherwood* Buddy Roosevelt, *Slater* John Bagni, *Thomas* Eddie Dew, *Truck henchman* George Allen, *Truck henchman* James Fawcett, *Dude Ward*

Al Taylor, *Man* Duke Green, *Man* Merlyn Nelson, *Man* Loren Riebc, *Man* David Sharpe, *Man* Cy Slocum, *Man* Tom Steele, *Man* Fenton "Duke" Taylor, *Man* Bill Wilkus, *Man* Joseph Yrigoyen.

Dick Tracy vs. Crime, Inc.
(January 1942)

Credits: *Executive producer* Herbert J. Yates, *Producer* William J. O'Sullivan, *Directors* William Witney, John English, *Screenplay* Ronald Davidson, Norman S. Hall, William Lively, Joseph O'Donnell, Joseph F. Poland, *Based on characters created by* Chester Gould, *Cinematography* Reggie Lanning, *Musical score* Cy Feuer, *"Make Yourself at Home" and "Swing Low Sweet Rhythm" music* Walter Bullock, *Lyrics* Jule Styne, *"Here Comes Romance" music* Raoul Kraushaar, *Lyrics* Peter Tinturin, *"Amor Espagnol" music* William Lava, *Art direction* John Victor Mackay, *Production manager* Allen Wilson, *Unit manager* Mack D'Agostino, *Supervising editor* Murray Seldeen, *Editors* Tony Martinelli, Edward Todd, *Special effects* Howard Lydecker, Theodore Lydecker, *Sound* Charles L. Lootens, Daniel J. Bloomberg, *Costumes* Robert Ramsey, Adele Palmer, *Makeup supervision* Robert Mark, *Location manager* John T. Bourke, *Set decoration* Morris Braun, *Construction supervisor* Ralph Oberg, *Casting* Robert Webb, *Optical effects* Consolidated Film Industries. Copyright 27 December 1941 (all chapters) by Republic Pictures Corporation; applied author: Republic Productions, Inc. RCA Photophone recording. Chapter 1, 30 minutes; all other chapters, 17 minutes each.

Chapter titles: 1–The Fatal Hour. 2–The Prisoner Vanishes. 3–Doom Patrol. 4–Dead Man's Trap. 5–Murder at Sea. 6–Besieged. 7–Sea Racketeers. 8–Train of Doom. 9–Beheaded. 10–Flaming Peril. 11–Seconds to Live. 12–Trial by Fire. 13–The Challenge. 14–Invisible Terror. 15–Retribution.

Rereleased on 8 October 1952 as *Dick Tracy vs. Phantom Empire*.

Cast: *Dick Tracy* Ralph Byrd, *J. P. Morton/The Ghost/Metzikoff* Ralph Morgan, *June Chandler* Jan Wiley, *Lucifer* John Davidson, *Lieutenant Cosgrove* Kenneth Harlan, *Henry Weldon* John Dilson, *Stephen Chandler* Howard Hickman, *Daniel Brewster* Robert Frazer, *Walter Cabot* Robert Fiske, *Jim Wilson* Jack Mulhall, *Arthur Trent* Hooper Atchley, *John Corey* Anthony Wade, *Trask* Chuck Morrison, *Billy Carr* Michael Owen, *Yard guard* Charles McMurphy, *Ranger* Julian Madison, *Police broadcaster* Douglas Evans, *Plant henchman* James Fawcett, *Plant henchman* Kenneth Terrell, *Plant henchman* Bob Robinson, *Plant henchman* Bud Geary, *Plant henchman* Al Seymour, *Plant henchman* Evan Thomas, *Plant henchman* Charley Phillips, *Pier henchman* David Sharpe, *Pier henchman* George Allen, *Pier henchman* Buddy Roosevelt, *Morgan* Walter Miller, *Jonathan Martin* C. Montague Shaw, *Inspector* John Webb Dillon, *House*

A rerelease ad for *Dick Tracy vs. Crime, Inc.*, retitled *Dick vs. Phantom Empire* (1952).

henchman Fred Kohler, Jr., *Drake* Terry Frost, *Arno Draga* Frank Alten, *Chuck/plant henchman* Bill Wilkus, *Chester* Barry Hays, *Army officer* Frank Meredith, *Watchman* Griff Barnette, *Riley* Howard Mitchell, *Pete* John Bagni, *Nick* Benny Burt, *Hideout henchman* Edwin Parker, *Driver* George Peabody, *Deck henchman/plant henchman* Fenton "Duke" Taylor, *Cigarette girl* Marjorie Kane, *Car henchman* Pat O'Shea, *Berke* Jack Kinney, *Vincent* Selmer Jackson, *Roof henchman* Wally Rose, *Patrol captain* Hugh Prosser, *Nurse* Carol Adams, *Marine captain/junction henchman* Walter McGrail, *Intern* William Hamner, *Dawson* Fred Schaefer, *Clancy* Charles McAvoy, *Canfield* Dick Lamarr, *Brownstone henchman* Raphael Bennett, *Brownstone henchman* Jacques Lory, *Brownstone henchman* Joseph Kirk, *Tom* Richard Rush, *Serviceman* Lynton Brent, *Operator* Frances Morris, *Launch henchman* Al Taylor, *Jackson* Stanley Price, *Henderson* Wheaton Chambers, *Ella Gilbert* Nora Lane, *Butler* Forrest Taylor, *Tim* Ray Hanson, *Slade* Sid Troy, *Kelly* Edmund Cobb, *Announcer* Archie Twitchell, *Helmsman* Robert J. Wilke, *Green* Sam Bernard, *Davis* John James, *Plant henchman/Pete Collins* Bert LeBaron, *Telegrapher* Max Maizman, *Smith* Alex Lockwood, *Junction henchman* Harry Tenbrook, *Junction henchman* Warren Jackson, *Grill room henchman* Bud Wolfe, *Cutter captain* Edward Hearn, *Customs inspector* Richard Kipling, *Brent* John Merton, *Hawes* Charles Miller.

Spy Smasher
(4 April 1942)

Credits: *Executive producer* Herbert J. Yates, *Producer* William J. O'Sullivan, *Director* William Witney, *Screenplay* Ronald Davidson, Norman S. Hall, Joseph F. Poland, William Lively, Joseph O'Donnell, *Story* Harrison Carter, *Based on characters created by* Ralph Daigh, Charles Clarence Beck, *Cinematography* Reggie Lanning, *Musical score* Mort Glickman, Arnold Schwarzwald, Paul Sawtell, *Orchestrations* Mort Glickman, Cy Feuer, Raoul Kraushaar, *Musical directors* Mort Glickman, Cy Feuer, *Special effects* Howard Lydecker, Theodore Lydecker, *Production manager* Max Schoenberg, *Unit manager* Mack D'Agostino, *Supervising editor* Murray Seldeen, *Editors* Tony Martinelli, Edward Todd, *Costumes* Robert Ramsey, Adele Palmer, *Makeup supervision* Robert Mark, *Art direction* John Victor Mackay, *Sound* Charles L. Lootens, Daniel J. Bloomberg, *Construction supervisor* Ralph Oberg, *Set decorations* Morris Braun, *Casting* Robert Webb, *Location manager* John T. Bourke, *Optical effects* Consolidated Film Industries. Copyright 4 April 1942 (all chapters) by Republic Pictures Corporation; applied author: Republic Productions, Inc. RCA Photophone recording. Chapter 1, 28 minutes; all other chapters, 17 minutes each.
    Chapter titles: 1–American Beware. 2–Human Targets. 3–Iron

From left, Kane Richmond and Frank Corsaro in *Spy Smasher* (1942).

Coffin. 4–Stratosphere Invaders. 5–Descending Doom. 6–The Invisible Witness. 7–Secret Weapon. 8–Sea Raiders. 9–Highway Racketeers. 10–2700° Fahrenheit. 11–Hero's Death. 12–V...–.

Released in a 100-minute feature version, *Spy Smasher Returns*, in 1966.

Cast: *Spy Smasher/Alan Armstrong/Jack* Kane Richmond, *Admiral Corby* Sam Flint, *The Mask* Hans Schumm, *Drake* Tristram Coffin, *Pierre Durand* Frank Corsaro, *Captain Gerhardt* Hans von Morhart, *Governor LeConte* Georges Renavent, *Colonel von Kohr* Robert O. Davis, *Ritter Lazar* Henry Zynda, *Lawlor* Paul Bryar, *Crane* Tom London, *Hayes* Richard Bond, *Dr. Hauser* Crane Whitley, *Steve* John James, *Eve Corby* Marguerite Chapman, *Walker* John Buckley, *Soldier* Roy Brent, *Soldier* Ray Hanson, *Soldier* Ray Jones, *Squadron leader* Tommy Coats, *Manager* Charles Regan, *Lumber henchman* Duke Green, *Policeman/Craig* Bud Wolfe, *Armored car driver* Enos "Yakima" Canutt, *Waiter* Pat Moran, *Squadron leader* Hugh Prosser, *Sniper* David Sharpe, *Joe* Louis Tomei, *Livingston* Ray Parsons, *Gerald Douglas* William Forrest, *Automobile clerk* Max Maizman, *Commandant* Buddy Roosevelt, *Valve sailor* Gilbert

Perkins, *Captain of storm troopers* Frank Altcn, *Sloan* Al Seymour, *Mechanic* Bert LeBaron, *Lieutenant* Leonard St. Leo, *Dungeon guard* Nick Vehr, *Chief operative* Robert J. Wilke, *Barn henchman* Howard Hughes, *Barn henchman* Charley Phillips, *Torpedo crew chief* Robert Stevenson, *Stuart* George J. Lewis, *Quartermaster* John Peters, *Pipe henchman* Bill Wilkus, *Pipe henchman* Loren Riebe, *Lewis/policeman* James Fawcett, *Storm trooper/Frtiz* Fenton "Duke" Taylor, *Captain* Martin Garralaga, *Blacksmith* Martin Faust, *Man* James Dale, *Man* Jack O'Shea, *Thornton* Arvon Dale, *Private* Cy Slocum, *Porter* Dudley Dickerson, *Launch henchman* Carey Loftin, *Gold henchman* Sid Troy, *Camera clerk* Jack Arnold, *Brick henchman* Tom Steele, *Brick henchman* Edward Jauregui, *Brick henchman* John Daheim, *Brick henchman* Bob Jamison, *Brick henchman* Walter Low, *Power clerk/Taylor* Carleton Young, *Burns* Jerry Jerome, *Jerry/storm trooper/policeman* Kenneth Terrell, *Guard* Lee Phelps, *Jailer* George Sherwood, *Head waiter* Lowden Adams.

Perils of Nyoka
(27 June 1942)

Credits: *Executive producer* Herbert J. Yates, *Producer* William J. O'Sullivan, *Director* William Witney, *Screenplay* Ronald Davidson, Norman S. Hall, William Lively, Joseph O'Donnell, Joseph F. Poland, Taylor Caven, *Based on characters created by* Edgar Rice Burroughs, *Cinematography* Reggie Lanning, *Musical score* Mort Glickman, Arnold Schwarzwald, *Musical directors* Mort Glickman, Walter Scharf, *Special effects* Howard Lydecker, Theodore Lydecker, *Production manager* Max Schoenberg, *Unit manager* Mack D'Agostino, *Supervising editor* Murray Seldeen, *Editors* Tony Martinelli, Edward Todd, *Art direction* Russell Kimball, *Set decorations* Otto Siegel, *Costumes* Robert Ramsey, Adele Palmer, *Makeup supervision* Ernest Westmore, *Sound* Charles L. Lootens, Daniel J. Bloomberg, *Process cinematography* Gordon Schaefer, *Sound effects* Herbert Norsch, *Dog owner and trainer* Earl Johnson, *Horse owner and trainer* Tony Campanero, *Construction supervisor* Ralph Oberg, *Casting* Robert A. Palmer, *Location manager* John T. Bourke, *Optical effects* Consolidated Film Industries. Copyright 27 June 1942 (all chapters) by Republic Pictures Corporation; applied author: Republic Productions, Inc. RCA Photophone recording. Chapter 1, 28 minutes; all other chapters, 17 minutes each.

Chapter titles: 1–Desert Intrigue. 2–Death's Chariot. 3–Devil's Crucible. 4–Ascending Doom. 5–Fatal Second. 6–Human Sacrifice. 7–Monster's Clutch. 8–Tuareg Vengeance. 9–Burned Alive. 10–Treacherous Trail. 11–Unknown Peril. 12–Underground Tornado. 13– Thundering Death. 14–Blazing Barrier. 15–Satan's Fury.

Rereleased on 2 April 1952 as *Nyoka and the Tigermen*. Released in a

Kay Aldridge in *Perils of Nyoka* (1942).

100-minute feature version, *Nyoka and the Lost Secrets of Hippocrates,* in 1966.

Cast: *Nyoka Gordon* Kay Aldridge, *Larry Grayson* Clayton Moore, *Red Davis* William Benedict, *Vultura* Lorna Gray, *Cassib* Charles B. Middleton, *Benito Torrini* Tristram Coffin, *Professor Douglas Campbell* Forbes Murray, *Professor Henry Gordon* Robert Strange, *John Spencer* George Pembroke, *Maghreb* Georges Renavent, *Lhoba* John Davidson, *Batan* George J. Lewis, *Ahmed/guard* Kenneth Terrell, *Yussuf* Leonard Hampton, *Hassan* Arthur Dupuis, *Ben Ali* John Bagni, *Tuareg leader* Bud Wolfe, *Tuareg* Enos "Yakima" Canutt, *Tuareg* Steve Clemente, *Tuareg* Dirk Thane, *Tuareg* Jerry Frank, *Tuareg* George Suzanne, *Tuareg* Duke Green, *Tuareg* Harry Smith, *Tuareg* Carey Loftin, *Tuareg* David Sharpe, *Tuareg* Jack O'Shea, *Tuareg* Cy Slocum, *Tuareg* George Plues, *Guard* Joe Garcia, *Guard* Loren Riebe, *Guard* Henry Wills, *Abou* Kenneth Duncan, *Translator* Forrest Taylor, *Ibrahim* Pedro Regas, *Brass worker* John Bleifer,

Bedouin Arvon Dale, *Bedouin* Augie Gomez, *Sidi* Robert Barron, *Nuri* Al Kikume, *Arab/Tuareg* John Daheim, *Satan* Emil Van Horn, *Reynolds* Herbert Rawlinson, *Arab* Iron Eyes Cody, *Arab/Tuareg/guard* Fenton "Duke" Taylor, *Arab/Tuareg/Riffi* Tom Steele, *Kay Aldridge's stunt double* Babe DeFreest, *Kay Aldridge's stunt double* Helen Thurston, *Fang [dog]* Ace, *Jitters [horse]* Professor.

King of the Mounties
(17 October 1942)

Credits: *Executive producer* Herbert J. Yates, *Producer* William J. O'Sullivan, *Director* William Witney, *Screenplay* Ronald Davidson, Joseph F. Poland, William Lively, Joseph O'Donnell, Taylor Caven, *Based on characters created by* Stephen Slesinger, Zane Grey, Romer Grey, *Cinematography* Ellis J. Thackery, *Process cinematography* Gordon Schaefer, *Musical score* Cy Feuer, *Orchestrations* William Lava, *Musical director* Mort Glickman, *Special effects* Howard Lydecker, Theodore Lydecker, *Production manager* Max Schoenberg, *Unit manager* Mack D'Agostino, *Supervising editor* Murray Seldeen, *Editors* Edward Todd, Tony Martinelli, *Art direction* Russell Kimball, *Set decorations* Otto Siegel, *Sound* Daniel J. Bloomberg, *Costumes* Robert Ramsey, Adele Palmer, *Makeup supervision* Ernest Westmore, *Sound effects* Herbert Norsch, *Location manager* John T. Bourke, *Casting* Robert A. Palmer, *Construction supervisor* Ralph Oberg, *Optical effects* Consolidated Film Industries. Copyright 17 October 1942 (all chapters) by Republic Pictures Corporation; applied author: Republic Productions, Inc. RCA Photophone recording. Chapter 1, 28 minutes; all other chapters, 17 minutes each.

Chapter titles: 1–Phantom Invaders. 2–Road to Death. 3–Human Target. 4–Railroad Saboteurs. 5–Suicide Dive. 6–Blazing Barrier. 7–Perilous Plunge. 8–Electrocuted. 9–Reign of Terror. 10–The Flying Coffin. 11–Deliberate Murder. 12–On to Victory.

Cast: *Sergeant Dave King* Allan "Rocky" Lane, *Commissioner Morrison* Gilbert Emery, *Marshal Carleton* Russell Hicks, *Carol Brent* Peggy Drake, *Professor Marshall Brent* George Irving, *Admiral Yamata* Abner Biberman, *Marshal von Horst* William Vaughn, *Count Baroni* Nestor Paiva, *Charles Blake* Bradley Page, *Gil Harper* Douglass Dumbrille, *Hall Ross* William Bakewell, *Pierre* Duncan Renaldo, *Zeke Collins* Francis Ford, *Lewis* Jay Novello, *Stark* Anthony Wade, *Radio announcer* Norman Nesbitt, *Lane* John Hiestand, *Sato* Allen Jung, *Japanese bombardier* Paul Fung, *Craig* Arvon Dale, *Man* David Sharpe, *Spike/Ord/lookout* Duke Green, *Ed Johnson* Hal Taliaferro, *Al* Kenneth Terrell, *Telegrapher* Forrest Taylor, *McGee* Stanley Price, *Joe* Earl Bunn, *Barn henchman* John Roy, *Barn henchman* Bud Weiser, *Smelter henchman* James Fawcett, *Mike* Tommy Coats, *Japanese pilot* Kam Tong, *Mountie/Becker/smelter*

Allan "Rocky" Lane in *King of the Mounties* (1942).

henchman Fenton "Duke" Taylor, *Shack henchman* Joe Chambers, *Brant* Frank Wayne, *Spike/Jack* Tom Steele, *Falcon pilot* Pete Katchenaro, *Road Japanese* Sam Serrano, *Road Japanese* King Kong, *Gus* Carleton Young, *Wade Garson* Harry Cording, *Plant guard* Jack Kinney, *Pete* Bob Jamison.

G-Men vs. the Black Dragon
(31 December 1942)

Credits: *Executive producer* Herbert J. Yates, *Producer* William J. O'Sullivan, *Directors* William Witney, John English, *Writers* Ronald Davidson, Joseph F. Poland, William Lively, Joseph O'Donnell, *Cinematography* Ellis J. Thackery, *Process cinematography* Gordon Schaefer, *Musical score* Mort Glickman, *Special effects* Howard Lydecker, Theodore Lydecker, *Production manager* Max Schoenberg, *Unit manager* Mack D'Agostino, *Supervising editor* Murray Seldeen, *Editors* Edward Todd, Tony Martinelli, *Art direction* Russell Kimball, *Set decorations* Otto Siegel, *Sound* Daniel J. Bloomberg, *Sound effects* Herbert Norsch, *Costumes* Robert Ramsey, Adele Palmer, *Makeup supervision* Ernest Westmore, *Construction supervisor* Ralph Oberg, *Casting* Robert A. Palmer, *Location manager* John T.

From left, Rod Cameron, Roland Got and George J. Lewis in *G-Men vs. the Black Dragon* (1942).

Bourke, *Optical effects* Consolidated Film Industries. Copyright 16 January 1943 (all chapters) by Republic Pictures Corporation; applied author: Republic Productions, Inc. RCA Photophone recording. Chapter 1, 26 minutes; all other chapters, 16 minutes each.

    Chapter titles: 1–The Yellow Peril. 2–Japanese Inquisition. 3–Arsenal of Doom. 4–Deadly Sorcery. 5–Celestial Murder. 6–Death and Destruction. 7–The Iron Monster. 8–Beast of Tokyo. 9–Watery Grave. 10–The Dragon Strikes. 11–Suicide Mission. 12–Dead on Arrival. 13–Condemned Cargo. 14–Flaming Coffin. 15–Democracy in Action.

    Released in a 100-minute feature version, *Black Dragon of Manzanar*, in 1966.

    Cast: *Rex Bennett* Rod Cameron, *Chang Singh* Roland Got, *Vivian March* Constance Worth, *Oyeme Haruchi* Nino Pipitone, *Ranga* Noel Cravat, *Luge* George J. Lewis, *Marie* Maxine Doyle, *Muller* Donald Kirk, *Customs inspector* Ivan Miller, *Williams* Walter Fenner, *Nicholson* C. Montague Shaw, *Tony Mills* Harry Burns, *James Kennedy* Forbes Murray, *Harrison J. Caldwell* Hooper Atchley, *Captain Gorman* Robert E. Homans, *Fugi* Allen Jung, *Airport announcer/newscaster* Norman Nesbitt, *Z-24*

An ad for *G-Men vs. the Black Dragon* (1942).

Eddie Dew, *Newsvendor* John Wallace, *Morse* Bud Geary, *Interceptor pilot* Charles Flynn, *House henchman* George DeNormand, *House henchman* Charley Phillips, *Balcony henchman* John Daheim, *Man* Otto Metzeth, *Warehouse henchman* Bud Wolfe, *Nick* Charles LaTorre, *Mill henchman* Martin Faust, *Mansion henchman/intern* Gilbert Perkins, *Graham* Walter Low, *John Brookfield* Lawrence Grant, *Turner* Elliott Sullivan, *Norris* Dick French, *Matron* Mary Bayless, *Jackson* William Forrest, *Gordon* Edward Keane, *Dale Burnell* Crane Whitley, *Tarner* Norman Willis, *Voice characterization of Tarner* Walter Thiel, *Nurse* Virginia Carroll, *Raymond Martin* John Hamilton, *Japanese captain/Japanese commander* Paul Fung, *Gibson* Pat O'Malley, *Butler* Edwin Parker, *Stewart* Edmund Cobb, *Pier henchman* Dale Van Sickel, *Truck henchman/mansion henchman* Fenton "Duke" Taylor, *Voice characterization of truck henchman* Buddy Roosevelt, *Jones* Ray Parsons, *Gabby Gibbs* Stanley Price, *Carl* Kenneth Terrell, *Spencer* Tom Seidel, *Pilot* Arvon Dale, *Laundry henchman* Eddie Phillips, *Laundry henchman* Bill Cody, *Garr* Peter George Lynn, *Casey/Lance* Kenneth Harlan, *Power clerk* John James, *Kettler* Robert Strange, *Voice characterization of Kettler* Baron Lichter, *Karl* Sam Bernard, *Garage henchman/intern* Tom Steele, *Crewman/seaman* Harry Tauvera.
Note: Sequel was *Secret Service in Darkest Africa* (1943).

Daredevils of the West
(1 May 1943)

Credits: *Executive producer* Herbert J. Yates, *Producer* William J. O'Sullivan, *Director* John English, *Writers* Ronald Davidson, Basil Dickey, William Lively, Joseph O'Donnell, Joseph F. Poland, *Cinematography* Ellis J. Thackery, *Process cinematography* Gordon Schaefer, *Musical score* Mort Glickman, *Musical director* Walter Scharf, *Special effects* Howard Lydecker, Theodore Lydecker, *Production manager* Max Schoenberg, *Unit manager* Mack D'Agostino, *Supervising editor* Murray Seldeen, *Editors* Wallace A. Grissell, Tony Martinelli, Edward Todd, *Art direction* Russell Kimball, *Set decorations* John McCarthy, Jr., Otto Siegel, *Sound* Daniel J. Bloomberg, *Costumes* Adele Palmer, Robert Ramsey, *Sound effects* Herbert Norsch, *Makeup supervision* Ernest Westmore, *Casting* William Stephens, *Location manager* John T. Bourke, *Construction supervisor* Ralph Oberg, *Optical effects* Consolidated Film Industries. Copyright 1 May 1943 (all chapters) by Republic Pictures Corporation; applied author: Republic Productions, Inc. RCA Photophone recording. Chapter 1, 26 minutes; all other chapters, 17 minutes each.
Chapter titles: 1–Valley of Death. 2–Flaming Prison. 3–The Killer Strikes. 4–Tunnel of Terror. 5–Firey Tomb. 6–Redskin Raiders. 7–Perilous Pursuit. 8–Dance of Doom. 9–Terror Trail. 10–Suicide Showdown. 11–Cavern of Cremation. 12–Frontier Justice.

From left, Allan "Rocky" Lane and Tom London in *Daredevils of the West* (1943).

Cast: *Duke Cameron* Allan "Rocky" Lane, *June Foster* Kay Aldridge, *Red Kelly* Eddie Acuff, *Barton Ward* William Haade, *Martin Dexter* Robert Frazer, *Silas Higby* Theodore Adams, *Turner* George J. Lewis, *Colonel Andrews* Stanley Andrews, *Sheriff Watson* Jack Rockwell, *Foster* Charles Miller, *Senator Garfield* John Hamilton, *Jim Brady* Budd Buster, *Commissioner* Kenneth Harlan, *George Hooker* Kenneth Duncan, *Jack* Rex Lease, *Indian chief* Chief Thundercloud, *Dave/bushwacker/Indian warrior/rustler/trail henchman* Duke Green, *Monk Mason/bushwacker/rock henchman/rustler/Jim* Edwin Parker, *Blue Eagle* Many Treaties, *T. M. Sawyer* Herbert Rawlinson, *Ed* Edmund Cobb, *Roustabout* Allen Pomeroy, *Barn henchman* Ray Jones, *Barn henchman* Rex Lease, *Joe/Bill/guard/barn henchman/rustler* Joseph Yrigoyen, *Bartender* Kenneth Terrell, *Indian warrior/Blackie/rustler/trail henchman* William Yrigoyen, *Marker/cave henchman* Tom Steele, *Townsman* Jack O'Shea, *Townsman* George Magrill, *Townsman* Earl Bunn, *Townsman* Pierce Lyden, *Townsman* George Plues, *Gulch henchman/townsman* Ralph Bucko, *Gulch henchman* Frank McCarroll, *Indian warrior/scalper* Augie Gomez, *Indian warrior* Rodric [Rodd] Redwing, *Indian warrior* Charles Brunner, *Indian warrior* Art Dillard, *Indian warrior* Warren Fiske, *Indian warrior* George Sky Eagle, *Indian warrior* Charles Soldani, *Indian warrior* George Sowards, *Indian warrior* Bryan Topetchy, *Indian warrior/townsman* Al Taylor, *Kaiga* Harry Smith, *Maxwell* Crane Whitley, *Miller* Tom London, *Powers* George Pembroke, *Man* Tex Cooper, *Man* Babe DeFreest, *Russell* Edward Cassidy.

Secret Service in Darkest Africa
(6 August 1943)

Credits: *Executive producer* Herbert J. Yates, *Producer* William J. O'Sullivan, *Director* Spencer Gordon Bennet, *Screenplay* Royal K. Cole, Basil Dickey, Jesse Duffy, Ronald Davidson, Joseph O'Donnell, Joseph F. Poland, *Based on characters created by* Ronald Davidson, Joseph F. Poland, William Lively, Joseph O'Donnell, *Cinematography* William Bradford, *Process cinematography* Gordon Schaefer, *Musical score* Mort Glickman, *Musical director* Walter Scharf, *Special effects* Howard Lydecker, Theodore Lydecker, *Production manager* Max Schoenberg, *Unit manager* Mack D'Agostino, *Supervising editor* Murray Seldeen, *Editors* Wallace A. Grissell, Thomas Malloy, *Sound* Earl Crain, Sr., Daniel J. Bloomberg, *Art direction* Russell Kimball, *Set decorations* John McCarthy, Jr., Otto Siegel, *Costumes* Robert Ramsey, Adele Palmer, *Makeup supervision* Ernest Westmore, *Sound effects* Herbert Norsch, *Casting* William Stephens, *Construction supervisor* Ralph Oberg, *Location manager* John T. Bourke, *Optical effects* Consolidated Film Industries. Copyright 6 August 1943 (chapters 1–5) and 18 August 1943 (chapters 6–10) (remaining chapters not

From left, Rod Cameron and Arab henchman in *Secret Service in Darkest Africa* (1943).

registered) by Republic Pictures Corporation; applied author: Republic Productions, Inc. RCA Photophone recording. Chapter 1, 26 minutes; all other chapters, 16 minutes each.

Chapter titles: 1–North African Intrigue. 2–The Charred Witness. 3–Double Death. 4–The Open Grave. 5–Cloaked in Flame. 6–Dial of Doom. 7–Murder Dungeon. 8–Funeral Arrangements Completed. 9–Invisible Menace. 10–Racing Peril. 11–Lightning Terror. 12–Ceremonial Execution. 13–Fatal Leap. 14–Victim of Villainy. 15–Nazi Treachery Unmasked.

Rereleased in 1954 as *Manhunt in the African Jungle*. Released in a 100-minute feature version, *The Baron's African War*, in 1966.

Cast: *Rex Bennett* Rod Cameron, *Janet Blake* Joan Marsh, *Pierre LaSalle* Duncan Renaldo, *Sultan Abou Ben Ali/Baron von Rommler* Lionel Royce, *Ernest Muller* Kurt Kreuger, *Wolfe* Frederic Brunn, *Luger* Sigurd Tor, *Armand* Georges Renavent, *Kurt Hauptmann* Kurt Katch, *Riverboat captain* Ralf Harolde, *Captain Boschert* William Vaughn, *Commandant* William Yetter, *First officer* Hans von Morhart, *Colonel van Raeder* Erwin Goldi, *Sir James Langley* Frederic Worlock, *Schloss* Frank Alten, *Hassan* Jack LaRue, *Sniper* Buddy Roosevelt, *Doctor* George Sorel, *Cafe henchman* Tom Steele, *Cafe henchman* John Daheim, *Ahmed Ali/ fireman/guard/lobby henchman/residence guard/Rakan* Kenneth Terrell, *Blacksmith* Bud Geary, *Abdul* Paul Marion, *Relzah* Anthony Warde, *Sheik* John Davidson, *Nazi officer* John Royce, *Emir* George DeNormand, *Karl Koche/cafe henchman* Edwin Parker, *Grave digger* Harry Semels, *Grave digger* Leonard Hampton, *Sailor/bushwacker/Rama/Fezal/guard/lobby henchman/Karl* Duke Green, *Bisra* Eddie Phillips, *Radio announcer* Norman Nesbitt, *Kaba* George J. Lewis, *Sufi* Charles LaTorre, *Zara* Emily LaRue, *Arab/workman* Carey Loftin, *Ray henchman/bushwacker/Arab/ lobby henchman/Wallah* Joseph Yrigoyen, *American officer* Reed Howes, *Fedallah* Walter Fenner, *Warehouse henchman* George Magrill, *Fireman* Jacques Lory, *Supply officer* Nino Bellini, *French officer* Ed Agresti, *French soldier* Jack Chefe, *Kasar* John Bleifer, *M-23* Augie Gomez, *Marga* Jack O'Shea.

Note: George Lucas has said this chapterplay was partial inspiration for *Raiders of the Lost Ark*.

The Masked Marvel
(6 November 1943)

Credits: *Executive producer* Herbert J. Yates, *Producer* William J. O'Sullivan, *Director* Spencer Gordon Bennet, *Writers* Royal K. Cole, Ronald Davidson, Basil Dickey, Jesse Duffy, Grant Nelson, George H. Plympton, Joseph F. Poland, *Cinematography* Reggie Lanning, *Process cinematography* Gordon Schaefer, *Musical score* Mort Glickman, Alberto Colombo, *Musical directors* Mort Glickman, Walter Scharf, *Special effects*

From left, Henchman and Tom Steele in *The Masked Marvel* (1943).

Howard Lydecker, Theodore Lydecker, *Production manager* Max Schoenberg, *Unit manager* George Webster, *Supervising editor* Murray Seldeen, *Editors* Earl Turner, Wallace A. Grissell, *Sound* Earl Crain, Sr., Daniel J. Bloomberg, *Art direction* Russell Kimball, *Set decorations* John McCarthy, Jr., Otto Siegel, *Costumes* Robert Ramsey, Adele Palmer, *Makeup supervision* Ernest Westmore, *Sound effects* Herbert Norsch, *Casting* William Stephens, *Construction supervisor* Ralph Oberg, *Location manager* John T. Bourke, *Optical effects* Consolidated Film Industries. Copyright 6 November 1943 (all chapters) by Republic Pictures Corporation; applied author: Republic Productions, Inc. RCA Photophone recording. Chapter 1, 26 minutes; all other chapters, 16 minutes each.

Chapter titles: 1–The Masked Crusader. 2–Death Takes the Helm. 3–Dive to Doom. 4–Suspense at Midnight. 5–Murder Meter. 6–Exit to Eternity. 7–Doorway to Destruction. 8–Destined to Die. 9–Danger Express. 10–Suicide Sacrifice. 11–The Fatal Mistake. 12–The Man Behind the Mask.

Released in a 100-minute feature version, *Sakima and the Masked Marvel*, in 1966.

Cast: *Martin Crane* William Forrest, *Alice Hamilton* Louise Currie, *The Masked Marvel/Cobb/estate henchman* Tom Steele, *Voice characteri-*

An ad for *The Masked Marvel* (1943).

zation of The Masked Marvel Gayne Whitman, *Mura Sakima* Johnny Arthur, *Jim Arnold* Rod Bacon, *Frank Jeffers* Richard Clarke, *Killer Mace* Anthony Warde, *Bob Barton* David Bacon, *Terry Morton* William Healy, *Warren Hamilton* Howard Hickman, *Plant guard* Kenneth Harlan, *Matthews* Thomas Louden, *Meggs* Edwin Parker, *Karl/Spike/Kaler* Duke Green, *Newscaster* Wendell Niles, *Reporter* Lester Dorr, *Reporter* Sam Ash, *Wilson* Ernest S. Adams, *Station henchman* Pat O'Shea, *Secretary* Nora Lane, *Karnes/Garnes* Joseph Yrigoyen, *Guard* Lynton Brent, *Guard* Lee Roberts, *Air raid warden* George Pembroke, *Watchman* Frank O'Connor, *J. D. Stone* Harold Kruger, *Ross/station henchman* Jack O'Shea, *Pete/Janson/Hart* Fred Graham, *Grail* Carey Loftin, *Barnes* Stanley Price, *Teamster* Bud Geary, *Teamster* Tom London, *Police sergeant* Sam Flint, *Kern* Roy Barcroft, *Gorton* Bill Cody, *Bartender* John Daheim, *Pier henchman* George Suzanne, *Kettering* Herbert Rawlinson, *Bert* Eddie Phillips, *Gas station attendant* Nolan Leary, *Photographer* Brooks Benedict, *A. M. MacRae* Edward Van Sloan, *Garage henchman* Robert J. Wilke, *Parsons* Harry Woods, *Philip Morton* George J. Lewis, *Kline/Bleek/Blunt* Dale Van Sickel, *Parker* Sam Bernard, *Foreman/dock henchman/bridge henchman* Kenneth Terrell, *Doctor* Forbes Murray, *Chef* Allan Pomeroy, *Curtiss* Crane Whitley, *Man* Charles Hutchison, *Man* Thom Metzetti, *Man* Preston Peterson, *Woman* Betty Miles.

Captain America
(January 1944)

Credits: *Executive producer* Herbert J. Yates, *Producer* William J. O'Sullivan, *Directors* John English, Elmer Clifton, *Screenplay* Royal K. Cole, Ronald Davidson, Basil Dickey, Jesse Duffy, Harry Fraser, Grant Nelson, Joseph F. Poland, *Based on characters created by* Joe Simon, Jack Kirby, *Cinematography* John MacBurnie, *Process cinematography* Gordon Schaefer, *Musical score* Mort Glickman, *Musical director* Walter Scharf, *Special effects* Howard Lydecker, Theodore Lydecker, *Production manager* Max Schoenberg, *Unit manager* Mack D'Agostino, *Supervising editor* Murray Seldeen, *Editors* Wallace A. Grissell, Earl Turner, *Sound* Ed Borschell, Daniel J. Bloomberg, *Costumes* Robert Ramsey, Adele Palmer, *Art direction* Russell Kimball, Fred A. Ritter, *Set decorations* John McCarthy, Jr., Charles Thompson, Otto Siegel, *Sound effects* Herbert Norsch, *Makeup supervision* Ernest Westmore, *Location manager* John T. Bourke, *Casting* William Stephens, *Optical effects* Consolidated Film Industries. Copyright 31 December 1943 (chapters 1–3), 23 February 1944 (chapters 4–10) and 5 February 1944 (chapters 11–15) by Republic Pictures Corporation; applied author: Republic Productions, Inc. RCA Photophone recording. Chapter 1, 26 minutes; all other chapters, 16 minutes each.

Chapter titles: 1–The Purple Death. 2–Mechanical Executioner. 3–

Dick Purcell in *Captain America* (1944).

The Scarlet Shroud. 4–Preview of Murder. 5–Blade of Wrath. 6–Vault of Vengeance. 7–Wholesale Destruction. 8–Cremation in the Clouds. 9–Triple Tragedy. 10–The Avenging Corpse. 11–The Dead Man Returns. 12–Horror on the Highway. 13–Skyscraper Plunge. 14–The Scarab Strikes. 15–The Toll of Doom.

Rereleased as *Return of Captain America.*

Cast: *Grant Gardner/Captain America* Dick Purcell, *Gail Richards* Lorna Gray, *Dr. Maldor/The Scarab* Lionel Atwill, *Commissioner Dryden* Charles Trowbridge, *Mayor Randolph* Russell Hicks, *Bart Matson* George J. Lewis, *Gruber* John Davidson, *Newscaster* Norman Nesbitt, *Professor*

Lyman Frank Reicher, *Professor Eldon Dodge* Hugh Sothern, *J. C. Henley* Tom Chatterton, *Dr. Clinton Lyman* Robert Frazer, *G. F. Hillman* John Hamilton, *Dirk* Crane Whitley, *Dr. Barace* Edward Keane, *Monk* John Bagni, *Simms* Jay Novello, *Booth/Agent 31* Paul Marion, *Airport mechanic* Lynton Brent, *Platinum henchman/Barton* Duke Green, *Woman* Helen Thurston, *Stark/Perry* Bert LeBaron, *Patrolman* Hal Craig, *Merritt* Charles Hutchison, *Mechanic henchman* George Magrill, *Garage henchman* Robert J. Wilke, *Bates* LeRoy Mason, *Florist* Brooks Benedict, *Florist* Sam Ash, *J. V. Wilson* James Carlisle, *Pete* George DeNormand, *Rick/ patrolman* Dale Van Sickel, *Morgue van driver* Glenn Knight, *Expressman* Jack Kirk, *Expressman* Jack O'Shea, *Blain/Burton/Mead* Fred Graham, *Walters/Walker* Allen Pomeroy, *Police broadcaster* Terry Frost, *Norden* Jeffrey Sayne, *Nick* Roy Brent, *Lewis/Burns* Joseph Yrigoyen, *Carl Evans* Herbert Lytoon, *Tait* Ralf Harolde, *Gas station attendant* Lorn Courdaye, *Mechanic* Harry Strang, *Car lot manager* Ben Erway, *Estate guard* Frank O'Connor, *Mack* Tom London, *Norton/Joe/Gordon* Gilbert Perkins, *Carson* Stanley Price, *Donovan* Ben Taggart, *Ed Graham* Kenneth Duncan, *Laboratory henchman* John Daheim, *Carter* Howard Hickman, *Detective* Post Parks, *Detective* Al Ferguson, *Gregory* Edward Van Sloan, *Kent* Tom Steele, *Clancy* George Sherwood, *Ewalt Davis* George Byron, *Kane* Bud Geary, *Guard* Edward Cassidy, *Hines* Robert Strange, *Road henchman/ laboratory henchman/Hunt* Kenneth Terrell, *Jarvis* Wilson Benge.

The Tiger Woman
(8 May 1944)

Credits: *Executive producer* Herbert J. Yates, *Producer* William J. O'Sullivan, *Directors* Spencer Gordon Bennet, Wallace A. Grissell, *Writers* Royal K. Cole, Ronald Davidson, Basil Dickey, Jesse Duffy, Grant Nelson, Joseph F. Poland, *Cinematography* Ellis J. Thackery, *Process cinematography* Gordon Schaefer, *Musical score* Joseph Dubin, *Musical director* Walter Scharf, *Special effects* Howard Lydecker, Theodore Lydecker, *General manager* Allen Wilson, *Unit manager* Mack D'Agostino, *Supervising editor* Murray Seldeen, *Editors* Harold A. "Heck" Minter, Earl Turner, *Sound* Thomas A. Carman, Daniel J. Bloomberg, *Art direction* Russell Kimball, Fred A. Ritter, *Set decorations* John McCarthy, Jr., Charles Thompson, *Costumes* Robert Ramsey, Adele Palmer, *Makeup supervision* Robert Mark, *Sound effects* Herbert Norsch, *Location manager* John T. Bourke, *Optical effects* Consolidated Film Industries. Copyright 8 May 1944 (chapters 1–6) and 27 June 1944 (chapters 7–12) by Republic Pictures Corporation; applied author: Republic Productions, Inc. RCA Photophone recording. Chapter 1, 25 minutes; all other chapters, 16 minutes each.

See the fabulous secrets of a tropical empire!

Hear an untamed white woman talk to wild beasts!

Feel the bone-chilling suspense when a white man breaks the law of the jungle!

PERILS
OF THE DARKEST JUNGLE
Formerly entitled "THE TIGER WOMAN"

A Republic Serial in 12 Chapters

with **ALLAN LANE**
LINDA STIRLING
DUNCAN RENALDO
GEORGE J. LEWIS
LeROY MASON
CRANE WHITLEY

Directed by Spencer Bennet — Wallace Grissell · Original Screen Play by Royal Cole — Ronald Davidson Basil Dickey — Jesse Duffy — Grant Nelson — Joseph Poland · Associate Producer — W. J. O'Sullivan

A reissue ad for *The Tiger Woman* retitled *Perils of the Darkest Jungle* (1951).

Chapter titles: 1–Temple of Terror. 2–Doorway of Death. 3–Cathedral of Carnage. 4–Echo of Eternity. 5–Two Shall Die. 6–Dungeon of the Doomed. 7–Mile a Minute Murder. 8–Passage to Peril. 9–Cruise to Cremation. 10–Target for Murder. 11–The House of Horror. 12–Triumph Over Treachery.

Working title was *The Tiger Woman of the Amazon*. Rereleased in

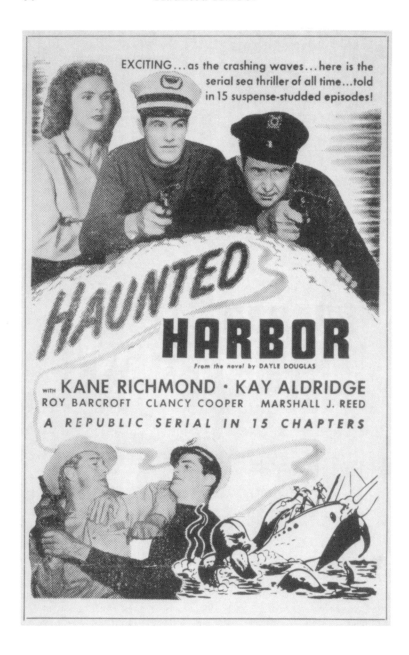

An ad for *Haunted Harbor* (1944).

1951 as *Perils of the Darkest Jungle*. Released in a 100-minute version, *Jungle Gold*, in 1966.

Cast: *Allen Saunders* Allan "Rocky" Lane, *The Tiger Woman* Linda Stirling, *Jose Delgado* Duncan Renaldo, *Morgan* George J. Lewis, *Fletcher Walton* LeRoy Mason, *Tom Dagget* Crane Whitley, *High Priest Ramgah* Robert Frazer, *Tegula* Rico de Montez, *Mack* Stanley Price, *Captain Scott* Nolan Leary, *Gentry* Kenneth Duncan, *Dumont* Tom London, *Lafe/ trooper/camp henchman/temple henchman/Rand* Cliff Lyons, *Temple henchman* Walt LaRue, *Flint/boat henchman/Grat/Fritz/Karnes* Duke Green, *Bartender* Charles Hayes, *Temple henchman/Lance/Largo/Karl* Tom Steele, *Travis/Blair/trooper/office henchman/guard/Gherkin* Edwin Parker, *Depot henchman/Bolton/Dixon/driver/Schlag* Kenneth Terrell, *Tony/blacksmith henchman* Bud Wolfe, *Pilot* Paul Gustine, *Blacksmith henchman* Bud Geary, *Blacksmith henchman* John Daheim, *Pete* Bert LeBaron, *Wilson* Herman Hack, *Road henchman/hill henchman* Robert J. Wilke, *Burt* Frank Marlowe, *Officer* Roy Darmour, *Slim* Carey Loftin, *Krantz/Roth/Frank* Dale Van Sickel, *Commandant* Georges Renavent, *Mart* Rex Lease, *Foster* Marshall J. Reed, *Goff/Hardin/Joe/Steve* Fred Graham, *Lon/hill henchman* Al Ferguson, *Man* Babe DeFreest, *Woman* Catherine McLeod, *Man* Joe Molina, *Man* Harry Smith, *Man* Augie Gomez.

Haunted Harbor
(18 August 1944)

Credits: *Executive producer* Herbert J. Yates, *Producer* Ronald Davidson, *Directors* Spencer Gordon Bennet, Wallace A. Grissell, *Screenplay* Royal K. Cole, Jesse Duffy, Grant Nelson, Joseph F. Poland, *Based on the novel by* Dayle Douglas [Ewart Adamson], *Cinematography* Ellis J. Thackery, *Process cinematography* Gordon Schaefer, *Musical score* Joseph Dubin, *Musical director* Walter Scharf, *Special effects* Howard Lydecker, Theodore Lydecker, *Unit manager* George Webster, *Supervising editor* Murray Seldeen, *Editors* Clifford Bell, Sr., Harold A. Minter, *Sound* Ed Borschell, Daniel J. Bloomberg, *Art direction* Russell Kimball, Fred A. Ritter, *Set decorations* John McCarthy, Jr., Perry Murdock, *Costumes* Adele Palmer, Robert Ramsey, *Makeup supervision* Robert Mark, *Sound effects* Herbert Norsch, *Location manager* John T. Bourke, *Optical effects* Consolidated Film Industries. Copyright 18 August 1944 (chapters 1–5), 14 September 1944 (chapters 6–10) and 12 October 1944 (chapters 11–15) by Republic Pictures Corporation; applied author: Republic Productions, Inc. RCA Photophone recording. Chapter 1, 25 minutes; all other chapters, 15 minutes each.

Chapter titles: 1–Wanted for Murder. 2–Flight to Danger. 3–Ladder of Death. 4–The Unknown Assassin. 5–Harbor of Horror. 6–Return of the

From left, Kenneth Duncan, Kay Aldridge and Bud Geary in *Haunted Harbor* (1944).

Fugitive. 7–Journey Into Peril. 8–Wings of Doom. 9–Death's Door. 10–Crimson Sacrifice. 11–Jungle Jeopardy. 12–Fire Trap. 13–Monsters of the Deep. 14–High Voltage. 15–Crucible of Justice.

Rereleased in 1951 as *Pirate's Harbor*.

Cast: *Jim Marsden* Kane Richmond, *Patricia Harding* Kay Aldridge, *Kane* Roy Barcroft, *Yank* Clancy Cooper, *Tommy* Marshall J. Reed, *John Galbraith* Oscar O'Shea, *Dr. Oliver Harding* Forrest Taylor, *Lawson* Hal Taliaferro, *Frederick Vorhees* Edward Keane, *Dranga* George J. Lewis, *Gregg* Kenneth Duncan, *Snell* Bud Geary, *Port captain* Robert E. Homans, *Grimes/guard/Kassam/Bert/rock henchman/Mead/Gort/Neville/ Denning* Duke Green, *Temil* Rico de Montez, *Bartender* Robert J. Wilke, *Stokes/barkeeper* Fred Graham, *Sailor/Taola* Kenneth Terrell, *Policeman* Richard Botiller, *Policeman* Frederic de Cordova, *Cave henchman* Bud Wolfe, *Cave henchman* Carey Loftin, *Chief* Nick Thompson, *Roustabout* Kit Guard, *Priest* Pietro Sosso, *Townsman* Charles Hayes, *Ronson/Clark/ guard/store henchman* Tom Steele, *Rock henchman* Jack O'Shea, *Duff/ guard/sailor* Dale Van Sickel, *Man* Herbert Evans, *Man* Edwin Parker, *Man* Harry Smith, *Man* Harry Wilson.

Zorro's Black Whip
(15 November 1944)

Credits: *Executive producer* Herbert J. Yates, *Producer* Ronald Davidson, *Directors* Spencer Gordon Bennet, Wallace A. Grissell, *Second unit director* Enos "Yakima" Canutt, *Screenplay* Basil Dickey, Jesse Duffy, Grant Nelson, Joseph F. Poland, *Story* Ruth Roman, *Based on characters created by* Johnston McCulley, *Cinematography* Ellis J. Thackery, *Process cinematography* Gordon Schaefer, *Musical director* Richard Cherwin, Walter Scharf *Special effects* Howard Lydecker, Theodore Lydecker, *Unit manager* George Webster, *Supervising editor* Murray Sledeen, *Editors* Clifford Bell, Sr., Harold A. Minter, *Sound* Ed Borschell, Daniel J. Bloomberg, *Art direction* Russell Kimball, Fred A. Ritter, *Set decorations* John McCarthy, Jr., Charles Thompson, *Costumes* Adele Palmer, Robert Ramsey, *Makeup supervision* Robert Mark, *Sound effects* Herbert Norsch, *Location manager* John T. Bourke, *Optical effects* Consolidated Film Industries. Copyright 15 November 1944 (chapters 1–6) and 26 December 1944 (chapters 7–12) by Republic Pictures Corporation; applied author: Republic Productions, Inc. RCA Photophone recording. Chapter 1, 23 minutes; all other chapters, 14 minutes each.

Chapter titles: 1–The Masked Avenger. 2–Tomb of Terror. 3–Mob Murder. 4–Detour to Death. 5–Take Off That Mask! 6–Fatal Gold. 7–Wolf

An ad for *Zorro's Black Whip* (1944).

Pack. 8–The Invisible Victim. 9–Avalanche. 10–Fangs of Doom. 11–Flaming Juggernaut. 12–Trail of Tyranny.

Cast: *Vic Gordon* George J. Lewis, *Barbara Meredith/The Black Whip II* Linda Stirling, *Tenpoint Jackson* Lucien Littlefield, *Dan Hammond* Francis McDonald, *Baxter* Hal Taliaferro, *Ed Harris* John Merton, *Walsh* John Hamilton, *Merchant* Tom Chatterton, *Commissioner James Bradley* Tom London, *Marshal* Jack Kirk, *Randolph Meredith/The Black Whip I* Jay Kirby, *Zeke Haydon* Si Jenks, *Hedges* Stanley Price, *Ed Hull/bushwacker/ attacker/townsman/Mack* Tom Steele, *Evans/Brown* Duke Green, *Danley/camp henchman/Karl* Dale Van Sickel, *Trail henchman* Vinegar Roan, *Mine henchman/trail henchman* Fenton "Duke" Taylor, *Mike/mine henchman* Kenneth Terrell, *Ambusher/rock henchman* Cliff Lyons, *Black* Fred Graham, *Bill Slocum* Robert J. Wilke, *Payne* Nolan Taylor, *Ed/trail henchman* Cliff Parkinson, *Townsman* Marshall Reed, *Townsman* Augie Gomez, *Townsman* Carl Sepulveda, *Townsman* Horace Carpenter, *Townsman* Herman Hack, *Attacker/Wagner* Roy Brent, *Becker* Forrest Taylor, *Rock henchman* Post Parks, *Dirk* Carey Loftin, *Burke/attacker* William Yrigoyen, *Man* Babe DeFreest.

Note: George J. Lewis continued his association with Zorro in *Ghost of Zorro* (1949) and the Disney teleseries *Zorro*.

Manhunt of Mystery Island
(13 January 1945)

Credits: *Executive producer* Herbert J. Yates, *Producer* Ronald Davidson, *Directors* Spencer Gordon Bennet, Wallace A. Grissell, Enos "Yakima" Canutt, *Writers* Albert DeMond, Basil Dickey, Jesse Duffy, Alan James, Grant Nelson, Joseph F. Poland, *Cinematography* Ellis J. Thackery, *Process cinematography* Gordon Schaefer, *Musical score* Richard Cherwin, *Musical director* Walter Scharf, *Special effects* Howard Lydecker, Theodore Lydecker, *Unit manager* R. G. Springsteen, *Supervising editor* Murray Seldeen, *Editors* Clifford Bell, Sr., Harold A. Minter, *Sound* Ed Borschell, Daniel J. Bloomberg, *Art direction* Russell Kimball, Fred A. Ritter, *Costumes* Adele Palmer, Robert Ramsey, *Makeup supervision*, Robert Mark, *Sound effects* Herbert Norsch, *Location manager* John T. Bourke, *Set decorations* John McCarthy, Jr., Charles Thompson, *Optical effects* Consolidated Film Industries. Copyright 13 January 1945 (chapters 1–5), 26 February 1945 (chapters 6–10) and 11 April 1945 (chapters 11–15) by Republic Pictures Corporation; applied author: Republic Productions, Inc. RCA Photophone recording. Chapter 1, 25 minutes; all other chapters, 14 minutes each.

Chapter titles: 1–Secret Weapon. 2–Satan's Web. 3–The Murder Machine. 4–The Lethal Chamber. 5–Mephisto's Mantrap. 6–Ocean Tomb. 7–The Death Drop. 8–Bombs Away. 9–The Fatal Flood. 10–The

Linda Stirling, henchman and Roy Barcroft in *Manhunt of Mystery Island* (1945).

Sable Shroud. 11–Satan's Shadow. 12–Cauldron of Cremation. 13–Bridge to Eternity. 14–Power Dive to Doom. 15–Fatal Transformation.

Released in a 100-minute feature version, *Captain Mephisto and the Transformation Machine*, in 1966.

Cast: *Lance Reardon* Richard Bailey, *Claire Forrest* Linda Stirling, *Captain Mephisto/Higgins* Roy Barcroft, *Sidney Brand* Kenneth Duncan, *Professor William Forrest* Forrest Taylor, *Henry Hargraves* Forbes Murray, *Edward Armstrong* Jack Ingram, *Fred Braley* Harry Strang, *Paul Melton* Edward Cassidy, *John Raymond* Frank Alten, *Reed* Lane Chandler, *Ruga* Russ Vincent, *Barker/Frazier/Lewis/Ritter/Sardon* Dale Van Sickel, *Lyons* Tom Steele, *Spencer Harvey/Clark* Duke Green, *C. D. Pembroke* Frederick Howard, *Joe Benson* Si Jenks, *Hill* Fenton "Duke" Taylor, *Blake* Fred Graham, *Captain/Fallon* Edwin Parker.

Federal Operator 99

(4 June 1945)

Credits: *Executive producer* Herbert J. Yates, *Producer* Ronald David-son, *Directors* Spencer Gordon Bennet, Wallace A. Grissell, Enos "Yakima" Canutt, *Writers* Albert DeMond, Basil Dickey, Jesse Duffy, Joseph F. Poland, *Cinematography* Ellis J. Thackery, *Process cinematog-raphy* Gordon Schaefer, *Musical directors* Richard Cherwin, Walter Scharf, *Special effects* Howard Lydecker, Theodore Lydecker, *Production manager* John E. Baker, *Unit manager* Roy Wade, *Supervising editor* Murray Sel-deen, *Editors* Clifford Bell, Sr., Harold A. Minter, *Sound* Victor Appel, Daniel J. Bloomberg, *Art direction* Russell Kimball, Fred A. Ritter, *Set decorations* John McCarthy, Jr., George Milo, *Makeup supervision* Robert Mark, *Costumes* Adele Palmer, Robert Ramsey, *Sound effects* Herbert Norsch, *Location manager* John T. Bourke, *Optical effects* Consolidated Film Industries. Copyright 4 June 1945 (chapters 1-6) and 6 July 1945 (chapters 7-12) by Republic Pictures Corporation; applied author: Republic Productions, Inc. RCA Photophone recording. Chapter 1, 22 minutes; all other chapters, 13 minutes each.

Chapter titles: 1–The Case of the Crown Jewels. 2–The Case of the Stolen Ransom. 3–The Case of the Lawful Counterfeit. 4–The Case of the Telephone Code. 5–The Case of the Missing Expert. 6–The Case of the Double Trap. 7–The Case of the Golden Car. 8–The Case of the In-vulnerable Criminal. 9–The Case of the Torn Blueprint. 10–The Case of the Hidden Witness. 11–The Case of the Stradivarius. 12–The Case of the Musical Clue.

Released in a 100-minute feature version, *F.B.I. 99*, in 1966.

Cast: *Jerry Blake* Marten Lamont, *Joyce Kingston* Helen Talbot, *Jim Belmont* George J. Lewis, *Rita Parker* Lorna Gray, *Matt Farrell* Hal Taliaferro, *Morton* LeRoy Mason, *Fred Martin* Bill Stevens, *Guiseppe Morello* Maurice Cass, *Tom Jeffries* Kernan Cripps, *Countess Delremy* Elaine Lange, *Warren Hunter* Frank Jaquet, *Otto Wolfe* Forrest Taylor, *Heinrick* Jay Novello, *Crawford* Tom London, *Riggs* Jack Ingram, *Duke/hood* Jack Kirk, *Corwin* Edmund Cobb, *Ed Atkins* Frederick Howard, *Nor-ton Corby* Kenneth Terrell, *Tony* Ernest S. Adams, *Johnny Daniels/Dor-gan/Gorman/Charles* Snyder/driver Tom Steele, *Austin* Craig Lawrence, *Lacy/Clay* Duke Green, *Solko* George Chesebro, *Hinds* Fred Graham, *Baker* Jack O'Shea, *Cashier* Nolan Leary, *Photographer* Curt Barrett, *Policeman/Joe* Walter Shumway, *Bank manager* Harry Strang, *Carlson/Sands/Sharon/Clark* Dale Van Sickel, *Messenger* Jimmy Zaner, *Mack* Frank Marlowe, *Roberto Carlotti* Jack George, *Benson* Michael Gaddis, *Monte Mason* Stanley Price, *Bower* Rex Lease.

Helen Talbot and Marten Lamont in *Federal Operator 99* (1945).

The Purple Monster Strikes
(3 August 1945)

Credits: *Executive producer* Herbert J. Yates, *Producer* Ronald Davidson, *Directors* Spencer Gordon Bennet, Fred C. Brannon, *Writers* Royal K. Cole, Jesse Duffy, Basil Dickey, Lynn Perkins, Joseph F. Poland, Barney A. Sarecky, *Cinematography* Ellis J. Thackery, *Process cinematography* Gordon Schaefer, *Musical directors* Richard Cherwin, Walter Scharf, *Special effects* Howard Lydecker, Theodore Lydecker, *Production manager* John E. Baker, *Unit manager* Roy Wade, *Supervising editor* Murray Seldeen, *Editors* Clifford Bell, Sr., Harold A. Minter, *Sound* Ed Borschell, Daniel J. Bloomberg, *Art direction* Russell Kimball, Fred A. Ritter, *Set decorations* John McCarthy, Jr., Jasper Cline, *Makeup supervision* Robert Mark, *Sound effects* Herbert Norsch, *Costumes* Adele Palmer, Robert Ramsey, *Location manager* John T. Bourke, *Optical effects* Consolidated

An ad for *The Purple Monster Strikes* (1945).

Film Industries. Copyright 3 August 1945 (chapters 1–6) and 11 October 1945 (chapters 7–15) by Republic Pictures Corporation; applied author: Republic Productions, Inc. RCA Photophone recording. Chapter 1, 22 minutes; all other chapters, 13 minutes each.

Chapter titles: 1–The Man in the Meteor. 2–The Time Trap. 3–Flaming Avalanche. 4–The Lethal Pit. 5–Death on the Beam. 6–The Demon Killer. 7–The Evil Eye. 8–Descending Doom. 9–The Living Dead. 10–House of Horror. 11–Menace from Mars. 12–Perilous Plunge. 13–Firey Shroud. 14–The Fatal Trail. 15–Take-Off to Destruction.

Released in a 100-minute feature version, *D-Day on Mars*, in 1966.

Cast: *Craig Foster* Dennis Moore, *Sheila Layton* Linda Stirling, *The Purple Monster* Roy Barcroft, *Dr. Cyrus Layton* James Craven, *Hodge Garrett* Bud Geary, *Marcia* Mary Moore, *Emperor of Mars* John Davidson, *Cal Stewart* John Whitehead, *Saunders* Emmett Vogan, *Paul Meredith* George Carleton, *Charley Mitchell* Kenneth Duncan, *Helen* Rosemonde James, *Harvey* Monte Hale, *Benjamin* Wheaton Chambers, *Workman* Robert J. Wilke, *Mack* Carey Loftin, *Andy Martin* Kenneth Terrell, *Evans* Robert Blair, *Baker/Curry/Ed Fletcher/Logan* Fred Graham, *Crandall* Frederick Howard, *Shaw* George Chesebro, *Osborne/Mason* Henry Wills, *Barnes* John Daheim, *Clay* Cliff Lyons, *Tony* Anthony Warde, *Policeman* Dale Van Sickel, *Fritz Benham/Joe/Mears* Tom Steele, *Woman* Polly Burson, *Man* Babe DeFreest.

Note: Sequels were *Flying Disc Man from Mars* (1951) and *Zombies of the Stratosphere* (1952).

The Phantom Rider
(26 October 1945)

Credits: *Executive producer* Herbert J. Yates, *Producer* Ronald Davidson, *Directors* Spencer Gordon Bennet, Fred C. Brannon, *Writers* Albert DeMond, Basil Dickey, Jesse Duffy, Lynn Roberts, Barney A. Sarecky, *Cinematography* Ellis J. Thackery, *Process cinematography* Gordon Schaefer, *Musical directors* Richard Cherwin, Walter Scharf, *Special effects* Howard Lydecker, Theodore Lydecker, *Production manager* John E. Baker, *Unit manager* Roy Wade, *Supervising editor* Murray Seldeen, *Editors* Clifford Bell, Sr., Harold R. Minter, *Sound* Victor Appel, Daniel J. Bloomberg, *Art direction* Russell Kimball, Fred A. Ritter, *Set decorations* John McCarthy, Jr., Allan Alperin, *Makeup supervision* Robert Mark, *Costumes* Adele Palmer, Robert Ramsey, *Sound effects* Herbert Norsch, *Location manager* John T. Bourke, *Optical effects* Consolidated Film Industries. Copyright 26 October 1945 (chapters 1–6) and 8 January 1946 (chapters 7–12) by Republic Pictures Corporation; applied author: Republic Productions, Inc. RCA Photophone recording. Chapter 1, 20 minutes; all other chapters, 13 minutes each.

From left, Dale Van Sickel, Peggy Stewart and Robert Kent in *The Phantom Rider* (1945).

Chapter titles: 1–The Avenging Spirit. 2–Flaming Ambush. 3–Hoofs of Doom. 4–Murder Masquerade. 5–Flying Fury. 6–Blazing Peril. 7–Gauntlet of Guns. 8–Behind the Mask. 9–The Captive Chief. 10–Beasts at Bay. 11–The Death House. 12–The Last Stand.

Rereleased in 1954 as *Ghost Riders of the West.*

Cast: *Dr. Jim Sterling/The Phantom Rider* Robert Kent, *Doris Shannon* Peggy Stewart, *Fred Carson* LeRoy Mason, *Blue Feather* George J. Lewis, *Ben Brady* Kenneth Duncan, *Nugget* Hal Taliaferro, *Yellow Wolf* Chief Thundercloud, *Cass* Monte Hale, *Ceta* Tom London, *Marshal* Roy Barcroft, *Senator Williams* John Hamilton, *Keeler* Hugh Prosser, *Turner* Jack Kirk, *Randall* Rex Lease, *Tim* Tommy Coats, *Attacker/Logan/ Blackie/bushwacker* Joseph Yrigoyen, *Lyons/Bart/Mack/Pete* Dale Van Sickel, *Renegade/lookout* William Yrigoyen, *Attacker/trail henchman* Bud Bailey, *Joe* Cactus Mack, *Renegade Indian* Robert J. Wilke, *Renegade Indian* John Roy, *Clay* Tom Steele, *Ace* Jack O'Shea, *Banker* George Carleton, *James Linn* James Linn, *Martin* Edwin Parker, *Dalton* George Chesebro, *Bushwacker* Walter LaRue, *Bushwacker* Carl Sepulveda, *Simpson* Hal Price, *Riot leader* Theodore Mapes, *Deputy marshal* Wayne Burson, *Indian henchman* Augie Gomez, *Attacker* Art Dillard, *Schwartz* Fenton "Duke" Taylor, *Indian guard* Bob Duncan, *Bushwacker/road henchman* Cliff Parkinson, *Dick* Cliff Lyons, *Tom/wagon driver* Post Parks, *Harry* Fred Graham, *Man* Tex Cooper, *Man* Henry Wills.

King of the Forest Rangers
(19 February 1946)

Credits: *Executive producer* Herbert J. Yates, *Producer* Ronald Davidson, *Directors* Spencer Gordon Bennet, Fred C. Brannon, *Writers* Basil Dickey, Jesse Duffy, Albert DeMond, Ronald Davidson, Lynn Perkins, *Cinematography* Ellis J. Thackery, *Process cinematography* Gordon Schaefer, *Musical directors* Raoul Kraushaar, Walter Scharf, *Special effects* Howard Lydecker, Theodore Lydecker, *Production manager* John E. Baker, *Unit manager* Roy Wade, *Supervising editor* Murray Seldeen, *Editors* Clifford Bell, Sr., Harold R. Minter, *Sound* Victor Appel, Daniel J. Bloomberg, *Art direction* Russell Kimball, Fred A. Ritter, *Set decorations* John McCarthy, Jr., Allan Alperin, *Makeup supervision* Robert Mark, *Costumes* Adele Palmer, Robert Ramsey, *Sound effects* Herbert Norsch, *Location manager* John T. Bourke, *Optical effects* Consolidated Film Industries. Copyright 19 February 1946 (chapters 1–6) and 8 April 1946 (chapters 7–12) by Republic Pictures Corporation; applied author: Republic Productions, Inc. RCA Photophone recording. Chapter 1, 20 minutes; all other chapters, 13 minutes each.

Chapter titles: 1–The Mystery of the Towers. 2–Shattering Evidence. 3–Terror by Night. 4–Deluge of Destruction. 5–Pursuit into

Henchman and Larry Thompson in *King of the Forest Rangers* (1946).

Peril. 6–Brink of Doom. 7–Design for Murder. 8–The Flying Coffin. 9–S.O.S. Ranger. 10–The Death Detector. 11–The Flaming Pit. 12–Tower of Vengeance.

Cast: *Steve King* Larry Thompson, *Marian Brennan* Helen Talbot, *Professor Carver* Stuart Hamblen, *Burt Spear* Anthony Warde, *Flush Haliday* LeRoy Mason, *Andrews/Bryan/Merkle/Sands* Scott Elliott, *Miner* Walter Soderling, *Rance Barton* Bud Geary, *Hank Harmon* Harry Strang, *Hiram Bailey* Ernest S. Adams, *Stover* Edwin Parker, *Holmes* Jack Kirk, *Martin/Al/Baker/Wade* Tom Steele, *Blaine/Hughes/Smith* Dale Van Sickel, *Harry Lynch* Stanley Blystone, *Mrs. Barton* Marin Sais, *Toler* Rex Lease, *Lee/Lang* Nick Warwick, *Brooks* Buddy Roosevelt, *Harbin* Joseph Yrigoyen, *Todd* James Martin, *Turner* Charles Sullivan, *Man* David Sharpe, *Hale* Jay Kirby, *Ronald Spencer* Wheaton Chambers, *Naylor* Kenneth Terrell, *Carleton* Robert J. Wilke, *Graham* Sailor Vincent, *Pilot* Bud Wolfe, *Townsman* Sam Ash, *Tom Judson* Tom London, *Forbes* Carey Loftin.

Daughter of Don Q
(4 June 1946)

Credits: *Executive producer* Herbert J. Yates, *Producer* Ronald Davidson, *Directors* Spencer Gordon Bennet, Fred C. Brannon, *Writers* Basil Dickey, Jesse Duffy, Albert DeMond, Lynn Perkins, *Cinematography* Ellis J. Thackery, *Process cinematography* Gordon Schaefer, *Musical directors* Raoul Kraushaar, Cy Feuer, *Special effects* Howard Lydecker, Theodore Lydecker, *Production manager* John E. Baker, *Unit manager* Roy Wade, *Supervising editor* Murray Seldeen, *Editors* Harold R. Minter, Clifford Bell, Sr., *Sound* Fred Stahl, Waldon O. Watson, *Art direction* Russell Kimball, Fred A. Ritter, *Set decorations* John McCarthy, Jr., Charles Thompson, *Makeup supervision* Robert Mark, *Costumes* Adele Palmer, Robert Ramsey, *Location manager* John T. Bourke, *Optical effects* Consolidated Film Industries. Copyright 4 June 1946 (chapters 1–6) and 19 July 1946 (chapters 7–12) by Republic Pictures Corporation; applied author: Republic Productions, Inc. RCA Photophone recording. Chapter 1, 20 minutes; all other chapters, 13 minutes each.

Chapter titles: 1–Multiple Murder. 2–Vendetta. 3–Under the Knives. 4–Race to Destruction. 5–Blackout. 6–Forged Evidence. 7–Execution by Error. 8–Window to Death. 9–The Juggernaut. 10–Cremation. 11–Glass Guillotine. 12–Dead Man's Vengeance.

Cast: *Dolores Quantaro* Adrian Booth, *Cliff Roberts* Kirk Alyn, *Carlos Manning* LeRoy Mason, *Mel Donavan* Roy Barcroft, *Maria Montenez* Claire Meade, *Grogan* Kernan Cripps, *Romero* Jimmy Ames, *George Thompkins* Edwin Parker, *Norton/Blake/Dow/Lyons* Tom Steele, *Murphy/Angus/Martin/Pete* Dale Van Sickel, *Rollins* Fred Graham, *R. J.*

From left, Roy Barcroft, Adrian Booth and George Chesebro in *Daughter of Don Q* (1946).

Riggs Thomas Quinn, *Morris Kelso* John Daheim, *Ned Gray* Theodore Mapes, *Lippy Moore* I. Stanford Jolley, *Moody/Zarco/Eddie* Buddy Roosevelt, *Philip Castilio* Frederick Howard, *Clay* George Chesebro, *Juan Perez* Jack O'Shea, *Walters* D'Arcy Miller, *Policeman* George Magrill, *Woman* Betty Danko, *Stone* Bud Wolfe, *Emilio Raymond* Eddie Rocco, *G-man* Michael Gaddis, *Rosa Peralta* Virginia Carroll, *Smith* Robert J. Wilke, *Shipping clerk* Matty Roubert, *Grogarty* Charles Sullivan, *Knockout Nellie* Maxine Doyle, *Sam Sloan* Kenneth Terrell, *Jake Simmons* Joseph Yrigoyen, *MacDuff* Arvon Dale.

The Crimson Ghost
(2 August 1946)

Executive producer Herbert J. Yates, *Producer* Ronald Davidson, *Directors* William Witney, Fred C. Brannon, *Writers* Albert DeMond, Basil Dickey, Jesse Duffy, Sol Shor, *Cinematography* Ellis J. Thackery, *Musical directors* Mort Glickman, Cy Feuer, *Special effects* Howard Lydecker, Theodore Lydecker, *Production manager* John E. Baker, *Unit manager* Roy

An ad for *The Crimson Ghost* (1946).

Wade, *Supervising editor* Murray Seldeen, *Editors* Harold R. Minter, Clifford Bell, Sr., *Sound* William E. Clark, Waldon O. Watson, *Art direction* Russell Kimball, Fred A. Ritter, *Set decorations* John McCarthy, Jr., Earl Wooden, *Makeup supervision* Robert Mark, *Hair styles* Peggy Gray, *Costumes* Adele Palmer, Robert Ramsey, *Sound effects* Mandine Rogne, *Location manager* John T. Bourke, *Optical effects* Consolidated Film Industries. Copyright 2 August 1946 (chapters 1–6) and 2 September 1946 (chapters 7–12) by Republic Pictures Corporation; applied author: Republic Productions, Inc. RCA Photophone recording. Chapter 1, 20 minutes; all other chapters, 13 minutes each.

    Chapter titles: 1–Atomic Peril. 2–Thunderbolt. 3–The Fatal Sacrifice. 4–The Laughing Skull. 5–Flaming Death. 6–Mystery of the Moun tain. 7–Electrocution. 8–The Slave Collar. 9–Blazing Fury. 10–The Trap That Failed. 11–Double Murder. 12–The Invisible Trail.

ColorImaged by American Film Technologies, Inc. in 1991. Released in a 100-minute feature version, *Cyclotrode X*, in 1966.

Cast: *Duncan Richards* Charles Quigley, *Diana Farnsworth* Linda Stirling, *Louis Ashe* Clayton Moore, *Blackton/voice characterization of The Crimson Ghost* I. Stanford Jolley, *Chambers* Kenneth Duncan, *Van Wyck* Forrest Taylor, *Anderson* Emmett Vogan, *Maxwell* Sam Flint, *Parker/The Crimson Ghost* Joe Forte, *Fator* Stanley Price, *Wilson* Wheaton Chambers, *Stricker/chauffeur/Karl* Tom Steele, *Harte/Carson* Dale Van Sickel, *Bain* Rex Lease, *Zane/Pete* Snyder Fred Graham, *Gross/Smith* Bud Wolfe, *Slim* Joseph Yrigoyen, *Cole* Bill Wilkus, *Mrs. Mallory* Rose Plummer, *Sherman* Edwin Parker, *Dikes* Kenneth Terrell, *Milt* William Yrigoyen, *Scott* Robert J. Wilke, *Ericson* Fenton "Duke" Taylor, *Nurse* Virginia Carroll, *Rosso* Rod Bacon, *Fiske* George Magrill, *Inspector* Richard Rush, *Kell* Eddie Rocco, *Palmer* Carey Loftin, *Kelly* John Daheim, *Logan* Loren Riebe, *Woman* Polly Burson.

Son of Zorro
(2 June 1947)

Credits: *Executive producer* Herbert J. Yates, *Producer* Ronald Davidson, *Directors* Spencer Gordon Bennet, Fred C. Brannon, *Screenplay* Franklyn Adreon, Basil Dickey, Jesse Duffy, Sol Shor, *Based on characters created by* Johnston McCulley, *Cinematography* Ellis J. Thackery, *Musical directors* Mort Glickman, Cy Feuer, *Special effects* Howard Lydecker, Theodore Lydecker, *Production manager* John E. Baker, *Unit manager* Roy Wade, *Supervising editor* Murray Seldeen, *Editors* Clifford Bell, Sr., Sam Starr, *Sound* William E. Clark, Waldon O. Watson, *Art direction* Russell Kimball, Fred A. Ritter, *Set decorations* John McCarthy, Jr., Perry Murdock, *Makeup supervision* Robert Mark, *Hair styles* Peggy Gray, *Costumes* Adele Palmer, Robert Ramsey, *Sound effects* Mandine Rogne, *Location manager* John T. Bourke, *Optical effects* Consolidated Film Industries. Copyright 2 June 1947 (all chapters) by Republic Pictures Corporation; applied author: Republic Productions, Inc. RCA Photophone recording. Chapter 1, 20 minutes; all other chapters, 13 minutes each.

Chapter titles: 1–Outlaw Country. 2–The Deadly Millstone. 3–Fugitive from Injustice. 4–Buried Alive. 5–Water Trap. 6–Volley of Death. 7–The Fatal Records. 8–Third Degree. 9–Shoot to Kill. 10–Den of the Beast. 11–The Devil's Trap. 12–Blazing Walls. 13–Checkmate.

Cast: *Jeff Stewart/Zorro* George Turner, *Kate Wells* Peggy Stewart, *Boyd* Roy Barcroft, *Sheriff Moody* Edward Cassidy, *Judge Hyde* Ernest S. Adams, *Pancho* Stanley Price, *Stockton* Edmund Cobb, *George Thomas*

George Turner and Peggy Stewart in *Son of Zorro* (1947).

Kenneth Terrell, *Caleb Baldwin* Wheaton Chambers, *Quirt* Fred Graham, *Melton* Si Jenks, *Fred* Jack O'Shea, *Hood* Jack Kirk, *Charlie/ Grimes/Blake* Tom Steele, *Murray/Dale/Forney/Kaw/Ted* Dale Van Sickel, *Auctioneer* Mike J. Frankovich, Sr., *Lem Carter* Pierce Lyden, *Louie Wells* Howard Mitchell, *Haskill/Hart* Bud Wolfe, *Van* John Daheim, *Haynes* Newton House, *Clark* Rocky Shahan, *Tom* George Chesebro, *Jailer* Frank O'Connor, *Raider/Green* Cactus Mack, *Cody* Theodore Adams, *Deputy sheriff/ sniper* Joe Phillips, *Larkin* Theodore Mapes, *Wagon driver* Post Parks, *Cole* Gilbert Perkins, *Raider* Herman Hack, *Raider/Lawton* Al Ferguson, *Dow* Charles L. King, *Cowman* Tex Terry, *Milt* Carl Sepulveda, *Jarvis/John Dixon* Fenton "Duke" Taylor, *Mark Daniels* Tom London, *Messenger* Tommy Ryan, *Deputy sheriff* Art Dillard, *Deputy sheriff* George Bell, *Man* Doc Adams, *Man* Pascale Perry, *Man* Tommy Coats, *Man* Joe Balch, *Man* Frank Ellis, *Man* Ralph Bucko, *Man* Roy Bucko, *Old man* Silver Harr.

Jesse James Rides Again
(2 June 1947)

Credits: *Executive producer* Herbert J. Yates, *Producer* Mike J. Frankovich, Sr. *Directors* Fred C. Brannon, Thomas Carr, *Writers* Franklyn Adreon, Basil Dickey, Jesse Duffy, Sol Shor, *Cinematography* John MacBurnie, *Process cinematography* Ellis J. Thackery, *Musical directors* Mort Glickman, Cy Feuer, *Special effects* Howard Lydecker, Theodore Lydecker, *Production manager* John E. Baker, *Unit manager* Roy Wade, *Supervising editor* Murray Seldeen, *Editors* Clifford Bell, Sr., Sam Starr, *Sound* Thomas A. Carman, Waldon O. Watson, *Art direction* Russell Kimball, Fred A. Ritter, *Set decorations* John McCarthy, Jr., James S. Redd, *Makeup supervision* Robert Mark, *Hair styles* Peggy Gray, *Costumes* Adele Palmer, Robert Ramsey, *Sound effects* Mandine Rogne, *Location manager* John T. Bourke, *Optical effects* Consolidated Film Industries. Copyright 2 June 1947 (all chapters) by Republic Pictures Corporation; applied author: Republic Productions, Inc. RCA Photophone recording. Chapter 1, 20 minutes; all other chapters, 13 minutes each.

Chapter titles: 1–The Black Raiders. 2–Signal for Action. 3–The

A reissue ad for *Jesse James Rides Again* (1947).

Stacked Deck. 4-Concealed Evidence. 5-The Corpse of Jesse James. 6-The Traitor. 7-Talk Or Die! 8-Boomerang. 9-The Captured Raider. 10-The Revealing Truth. 11-Black Gold. 12-Deadline at Midnight.

Cast: *Jesse James* Clayton Moore, *Ann Bolton* Linda Stirling, *Frank Lawton* Roy Barcroft, *Steve Lane* John Compton, *James Clark* Tristram Coffin, *Sam Bolton* Tom London, *Tim* Holly Bane, *Wilkie* Edmund Cobb, *Sheriff Duffie* Gene Stutenroth [Gene Roth], *Amos Hawks* Fred Graham, *Grant* Edward Cassidy, *Sam* Dave Anderson, *Captain Flint* Edwin Parker, *Goff/Bates/Cole* Tom Steele, *Raider/Brock/Boyd/Gow/Hood* Dale Van Sickel, *Finley* LeRoy Mason, *Barkeeper* Robert Blair, *Dale/Bass* Theodore Mapes, *Wynn* Keith Richards, *Blair* Tex Terry, *Lafe* Charles Roberson, *First Joe* Frank Marlowe, *Second Joe/Kaw* Herman Hack, *Mort* Carl Sepulveda, *Clem Williams* Richard Alexander, *Cody* Gilbert Perkins, *Haynes* Loren Riebe, *Ward* Howard Mitchell, *Price* Kenneth Terrell, *Doty* Tex "Squint" Palmer, *Harlan* Carey Loftin, *Waldon* Robert Riordan, *Raider* Bert LeBaron, *Raider* Pascale Perry, *Trent* Charles L. King, *Jim Doyle* Casey MacGregor, *Hammond* Lee Shumway, *Drunk* Emmett Lynn, *Rose* Nellie Walker, *Mack Tobin* Tom Chatterton, *Farmer* Charles Morton, *Farmer* Watson Downs, *Roy* Chester Conklin, *Stock* Bud Wolfe, *Gil* Fenton "Duke" Taylor, *Green* Monte Montague, *Gus Simmons* George Chesebro, *Saloon patron* Tommy Coats, *Woman* Helen Griffith, *Man* Don Summers, *Man* Victor Cox.

Note: Sequels were *Adventures of Frank and Jesse James* (1948) and *The James Brothers of Missouri* (1950).

The Black Widow
(28 July 1947)

Credits: *Executive producer* Herbert J. Yates, *Producer* Mike J. Frankovich, Sr., *Directors* Spencer Gordon Bennet, Fred C. Brannon, *Writers* Franklyn Adreon, Basil Dickey, Jesse Duffy, Sol Shor, *Cinematography* John MacBurnie, *Process cinematography* Ellis J. Thackery, *Musical directors* Mort Glickman, Cy Feuer, *Special effects* Howard Lydecker, Theodore Lydecker, *Production manager* John E. Baker, *Unit manager* Roy Wade, *Supervising editor* Murray Seldeen, *Editors* Clifford Bell, Sr., Sam Starr, *Sound* Herbert Norsch, Waldon O. Watson, *Art direction* Russell Kimball, Fred A. Ritter, *Set decorations* John McCarthy, Jr., James S. Redd, *Makeup supervision* Robert Mark, *Hair styles* Peggy Gray, *Costumes* Adele Palmer, Robert Ramsey, *Sound effects* Mandine Rogne, *Location manager* John T. Bourke, *Optical effects* Consolidated Film Industries. Copyright 28 July 1947 (chapters 1–5) and 2 September 1947 (chapters 6–13) by Republic Pictures Corporation; applied author: Republic Productions, Inc. RCA Photophone recording. Chapter 1, 20 minutes; all other chapters, 13 minutes each.

A
REPUBLIC SERIAL
IN 13 CHAPTERS

THE
BLACK
WIDOW

featuring BRUCE EDWARDS
VIRGINIA LINDLEY
CAROL FORMAN
ANTHONY WARDE

An ad for *The Black Widow* (1947).

Chapter titles: 1–Deadly Prophecy. 2–The Stolen Formula. 3–Hidden Death. 4–Peril in the Sky. 5–The Spider's Lair. 6–The Glass Guillotine. 7–Wheels of Death. 8–False Information. 9–The Spider's Venom. 10–The Stolen Corpse. 11–Death Dials a Number. 12–The Talking Mirror. 13–A Life for a Life.

Released in a 100-minute feature version, *Sombra the Spider Woman*, in 1966.

Cast: *Steve Colt* Bruce Edwards, *Joyce Winters* Virginia Lindley, *Sombra* Carol Forman, *Nick Ward* Anthony Warde, *Ruth Dayton* Ramsay Ames, *Z. V. Jaffa* I. Stanford Jolley, *Hitomu* Theodore Gottlieb, *Dr. Ann Curry* Virginia Carroll, *John M. Walker* Gene Stutenroth [Gene Roth], *Henry Weston* Sam Flint, *Bard/Blair/Jack* Tom Steele, *Bill/Bass/Hodges/ Smith* Dale Van Sickel, *Dr. Godfrey* LeRoy Mason, *Trixie* Laura Stevens, *Triangulator* Arvon Dale, *Triangulator* John Alban, *Bradley* Forrest Taylor, *Spike* Carey Loftin, *Link* Robert Barron, *Blinkey* Ernest S. Adams, *Finnegan* Jack O'Shea, *Nurse MacIntyre* Peggy Wayne, *Slade* Theodore Mapes, *Michael Burns* Keith Richards, *Detective* Bob Reeves, *Lee* Frank White, *Mark* John Phillips, *Fortune teller* Maxine Doyle, *Reporter* Jerry Jerome, *Reporter* Richard Gordon, *Mendoza* Kenneth Terrell, *Kabob* Frank Lackteen, *Guard* Bud Wolfe, *Carter* George Chesebro, *Andy Baldwin* Hal Landon, *Porter* Dave Anderson, *Ted Mills* Duke Green, *Inspector* Frank O'Connor, *Fillmore Hagin* Stanley Price, *Burke* Gilbert Perkins, *Jailer/taxi driver* Robert J. Wilke, *Policeman* Charles Sullivan, *Harris* George Douglas, *Morgue attendant* Bill Bailey, *Harcourt* Larry Steers.

G-Men Never Forget
(13 November 1947)

Credits: *Executive producer* Herbert J. Yates, *Producer* Mike J. Frankovich, Sr., *Directors* Fred C. Brannon, Enos "Yakima" Canutt, *Writers*

Franklyn Adreon, Basil Dickey, Jesse Duffy, Sol Shor, *Cinematography* John MacBurnie, *Process cinematography* Ellis J. Thackery, *Musical directors* Mort Glickman, Cy Feuer, *Special effects* Howard Lydecker, Theodore Lydecker, *Production manager* John E. Baker, *Unit manager* Roy Wade, *Supervising editor* Murray Seldeen, *Editors* Clifford Bell, Sr., Sam Starr, *Sound* Garry A. Harris, Waldon O. Watson, *Art direction* Russell Kimball, Frank Arrigo, *Set decorations* John McCarthy, Jr., James S. Redd, *Makeup supervision* Robert Mark, *Hair styles* Peggy Gray, *Costumes* Adele Palmer, Robert Ramsey, *Sound effects* Mandine Rogne, *Location manager* John T. Bourke, *Optical effects* Consolidated Film Industries. Copyright 13 November 1947) (chapters 1–6) and 21 November 1947 (chapters 7–12) by Republic Pictures Corporation; applied author: Republic Productions, Inc. RCA Photophone recording. Chapter 1, 20 minutes; all other chapters, 13 minutes each.

Chapter titles: 1–Death Rides the Torrent. 2–The Flaming Doll House. 3–Code 6-4-5. 4–Shipyard Saboteurs. 5–The Dead Man Speaks. 6–Marked Money. 7–Hot Cargo. 8–The Fatal Letter. 9–The Death Wind. 10– The Innocent Victim. 11–Counter-Plot. 12–Exposed.

Released in a 100-minute feature version, *Code 6-4-5*, in 1966.

Cast: *Ted O'Hara* Clayton Moore, *Victor Murkland/Angus*

An ad for *G-Men Never Forget* (1947).

Cameron Roy Barcroft, *Frances Blake* Ramsay Ames, *Duke Graham* Drew Allen, *Parker/Gifford/Jack* Tom Steele, *Fred Brent/Bud/Gil/Pete/Slocum/Wilkins* Dale Van Sickel, *R. J. Cook* Edmund Cobb, *Robert Benson*

Stanley Price, *Slater* Jack O'Shea, *George* Barry Brooks, *Hayden* Douglas Aylesworth, *District Attorney McLain* Frank O'Connor, *Miss Stewart* Dian Fauntelle, *Fiddler* Eddie Acuff, *Staley* George Magrill, *John Kelsey/Bert/First Joe* Kenneth Terrell, *Second Joe* Tom Monroe, *Vance/Trent* David Sharpe, *Al* Tom McDonough, *Steele* Robert J. Wilke, *Hodge* Carey Loftin, *Bailey* James Linn, *Roberts* Phil Warren, *Hinkey* Charles Regan, *Baxter* Russ Whitman, *Nichols* Duke Green, *Guard* George Douglas, *Dale* John Crawford, *Morgan* Charles Sullivan, *Garson* Robert Barron, *Dorsey* Glenn Turner, *Moore* Arvon Dale, *Foy* Bud Wolfe, *Finch* Gilbert Perkins, *Kramer* John Daheim, *Foreman* Matty Roubert.

Dangers of the Canadian Mounted
(17 February 1948)

Credits: *Executive producer* Herbert J. Yates, *Producer* Mike J. Frankovich, Sr., *Directors* Fred C. Brannon, Enos "Yakima" Canutt, *Writers*

A reissue ad for *Dangers of the Canadian Mounted* (1948).

Franklyn Adreon, Basil Dickey, Jesse Duffy, Sol Shor, Robert G. Walker, *Cinematography* John MacBurnie, *Process cinematography* Ellis J. Thackery, *Musical directors* Mort Glickman, Cy Feuer, *Special effects* Howard Lydecker, Theodore Lydecker, *Production manager* John E. Baker, *Unit manager* Roy Wade, *Art direction* Russell Kimball, Fred A. Ritter, *Set decorations* John McCarthy, Jr., James S. Redd, *Supervising editor* Murray Seldeen, *Editors* Clifford Bell, Sr., Sam Starr, *Sound* Earl Crain, Sr., Waldon O. Watson, *Makeup supervision* Robert Mark, *Hair styles* Peggy Gray, *Costumes* Adele Palmer, Robert Ramsey, *Sound effects* Mandine Rogne, *Location manager* John T. Bourke, *Optical effects* Consolidated Film Industries. Copyright 17 February 1948 (all chapters) by Republic Pictures Corporation; applied author: Republic Productions, Inc. RCA Photophone recording. Chapter 1, 20 minutes; all other chapters, 13 minutes each.

Chapter titles: 1–Legend of Genghis Khan. 2–Key to the Legend. 3–Ghost Town. 4–Terror in the Sky. 5–Pursuit. 6–Stolen Cargo. 7–The Fatal Shot. 8–Fatal Testimony. 9–The Prisoner Spy. 10–The Secret Meeting. 11–Secret of the Altar. 12–Liquid Jewels.

Released in a 100-minute feature version, *R.C.M.P. and the Treasure of Genghis Khan*, in 1966.

Cast: *Christopher Royal* Jim Bannon, *Bobbie Page* Virginia Belmont, *Mort Fowler* Anthony Warde, *Skagway Kate* Dorothy Granger, *Dan Page* Bill Van Sickel, *Fagin/Carter/driver/Lou/Sloan/Spike* Tom Steele, *Boyd/ Bart/Pete/Scott/Steele* Dale Van Sickel, *J. P. Belanco* I. Stanford Jolley, *George Hale* Phil Warren, *Dale* Lee Morgan, *Andy Knight* James Dale, *Meggs* Theodore Adams, *Danton* John Crawford, *Marshal* Jack Clifford, *Lowry* Edwin Parker, *Commissioner Barton* Frank O'Connor, *Martin Addison* James Carlisle, *Ray Watson* Arvon Dale, *Art/Curry/Fenton/Grady/ guard/Masters/Tom* Kenneth Terrell, *Zeke/Vance* Bud Wolfe, *Baker* Eddie Phillips, *Track thug* Al Taylor, *Track thug* Harry Cording, *Baxter* Robert J. Wilke, *A. L. Thomas* Jack Kirk, *Porter/clerk* Carey Loftin, *Ralph* Charles Regan, *Joe/Williams/Douglas/Dave* Marshall Reed, *Mack* Theodore Mapes, *Ford* House Peters, Jr., *Ken* Paul Gustine, *Frank* Tom McDonough, *Garson* Holly Bane, *Radio announcer* Donald "Red" Barry, *Radio announcer* Roy Barcroft.

Adventures of Frank and Jesse James
(August 1948)

Credits: *Executive producer* Herbert J. Yates, *Producer* Franklyn Adreon, *Directors* Fred C. Brannon, Enos "Yakima" Canutt, *Writers* Basil Dickey, Franklyn Adreon, Sol Shor, Robert G. Walker, *Cinematography* John MacBurnie, *Process cinematography* Ellis J. Thackery, *Musical director* Morton Scott, *Special effects* Howard Lydecker, Theodore Lydecker,

A reissue ad for *Adventures of Frank and Jesse James* (1948).

Production manager John E. Baker, *Unit manager* Roy Wade, *Art direction* Ralph Oberg, Fred A. Ritter, *Set decorations* John McCarthy, Jr., Charles Thompson, *Supervising editor* Murray Seldeen, *Editors* Clifford Bell, Sr., Sam Starr, *Sound* Earl Crain, Sr., Waldon O. Watson, *Makeup supervision* Robert Mark, *Hair styles* Peggy Gray, *Costumes* Adele Palmer, Robert Ramsey, *Sound effects* Mandine Rogne, *Location manager* John T. Bourke, *Casting* Jack Grant, *Optical effects* Consolidated Film Industries. Copyright 26 July 1948 (chapters 1–7) and 12 November 1948 (chapters 8–13) by Republic Pictures Corporation; applied author: Republic Productions, Inc. RCA Photophone recording. Chapter 1, 20 minutes; all other chapters, 13 minutes each.

Chapter titles: 1–Agent of Treachery. 2–The Hidden Witness. 3–The Lost Tunnel. 4–Blades of Death. 5–Roaring Wheels. 6–Passage to Danger. 7–The Secret Code. 8–Doomed Cargo. 9–The Eyes of the Law. 10–The Stolen Body. 11–Suspicion. 12–Talk or Die! 13–Unmasked.

Cast: *Jesse James* Clayton Moore, *Frank James* Steve Darrell, *Judy Powell* Noel Neill, *Rafe Henley* George J. Lewis, *Jim Powell* Stanley Andrews, *Amos Ramsey* John Crawford, *Paul Thatcher* Sam Flint, *Sheriff Towey* House Peters, Jr. *Thomas Dale/Art Carter/Jones* Dale Van Sickel, *Mike Steele/Barton/Gus* Tom Steele, *J. B. Nichols* James Dale, *Ward I.* Stanford Jolley, *Marshal* Gene Stutenroth [Gene Roth], *Bill* Lane Bradford, *Jim* George Chesebro, *Casey* Jack Kirk, *Sheriff Barton* Steve Clark, *Zeb* Kenneth Terrell, *Bull* Fenton "Duke" Taylor, *Tim* Bob Reeves, *Pete/Carlson* Carey Loftin, *Seth* David Sharpe, *Carver* Duke Green, *Rosita* Rosa Turich, *Davin* Ralph Bucko, *Moody* Bud Wolfe, *Dick* Victor Cox, *Bat Kelsey* Bud Osborne, *First Dirk* Fred Graham, *Second Dirk* Guy Teague, *Jergens/Joe* Edwin Parker, *Doctor* Frank O'Connor, *Hall* Augie Gomez, *Grady* Joseph Yrigoyen, *Man* Joe Phillips, *Townsman* Frank Ellis, *Townsman* Art Dillard, *Townsman* Roy Bucko.

Federal Agents vs. Underworld, Inc.
(12 November 1948)

Credits: *Executive producer* Herbert J. Yates, *Producer* Franklyn Adreon, *Director* Fred C. Brannon, *Writers* Basil Dickey, Sol Shor, Royal K. Cole, William Lively, *Cinematography* John MacBurnie, *Process cinematography* Ellis J. Thackery, *Musical score* Stanley Wilson, *Musical director* Morton Scott, *Special effects* Howard Lydecker, Theodore Lydecker, *Production manager* John E. Baker, *Unit manager* Roy Wade, *Art direction* Ralph Oberg, Fred A. Ritter, *Set decorations* John McCarthy, Jr., James S. Redd, *Supervising editor* Murray Seldeen, *Editors* Clifford Bell, Sr., Sam Starr, *Sound* Earl Crain, Sr., Waldon O. Watson, *Costumes* Adele Palmer, Robert Ramsey, *Makeup supervision* Robert Mark, *Hair styles* Peggy Gray, *Sound effects* Mandine Rogne, *Location manager* John T. Bourke, *Casting* Jack Grant, *Optical effects* Consolidated Film Industries. Copyright 12 November 1948 (chapters 1–6) and 8 December 1948 (chapters 7–12) by Republic Pictures Corporation; applied author: Republic Productions, Inc. RCA Photophone recording. Chapter 1, 20 minutes; all other chapters, 13 minutes each.

Chapter titles: 1–The Golden Hands. 2–The Floating Coffin. 3–Death in the Skies. 4–Fatal Evidence. 5–The Trapped Conspirator. 6–Wheels of Disaster. 7–The Hidden Key. 8–The Enemy's Mouthpiece. 9–The Stolen Hand. 10–Unmasked. 11–Tombs of the Ancients. 12–The Curse of Kurigal.

Released in a 100-minute feature version, *Golden Hands of Kurigal*, in 1966.

Cast: *Dave Worth* Kirk Alyn, *Laura Keith* Rosemary LaPlanche, *Spade Gordon* Roy Barcroft, *Nila* Carol Forman, *Steve Evans* James Dale, *Professor Paul Williams* Bruce Edwards, *Professor James Clayton* James

From left, Kirk Alyn, Roy Barcroft and Tom Steele in *Federal Agents vs. Underworld, Inc.* (1948).

Craven, *Frank Chambers* Tristram Coffin, *Tim Grey/native/Larkin/Haskell/Mort* Tom Steele, *Professor Elwood M. Graves* James Carlisle, *Ali* Jack O'Shea, *O'Hara* Marshall Reed, *Zod* Robert J. Wilke, *Native* Robert St. Angelo, *Native* Art Dillard, *Native* David Sharpe, *Porter* Dave Anderson, *Guard/Mack* Dale Van Sickel, *Black/Dorsey* Carey Loftin, *Bleck* Post Parks, *Carson/Native* Joseph Yrigoyen, *Corby* Bud Wolfe, *Digger* Saul Gorss, *Digger* Loren Riebe, *Guard* John Daheim, *Karnak* Bert LeBaron, *Native/Maston* Fenton "Duke" Taylor, *Murdock* Kenneth Terrell.

Ghost of Zorro
(12 April 1949)

Credits: *Executive producer* Herbert J. Yates, *Producer* Franklyn Adreon, *Director* Fred C. Brannon, *Screenplay* Royal K. Cole, William Lively, Sol Shor, *Based on characters created by* Johnston McCulley, *Cinematography* John MacBurnie, *Process cinematography* Ellis J. Thackery, *Musical score* Stanley Wilson, *Musical director* Morton Scott, *Special effects* Howard Lydecker, Theodore Lydecker, *Production manager*

Clayton Moore and Pamela Blake in *Ghost of Zorro* (1949).

John E. Baker, *Unit manager* Roy Wade, *Art direction* Ralph Oberg, Fred A. Ritter, *Set decorations* John McCarthy, Jr., James S. Redd, *Supervising editor* Murray Seldeen, *Editors* Clifford Bell, Sr., Harold A. Minter, *Sound* Richard Tyler, Waldon O. Watson, *Makeup supervision* Robert Mark, *Hair styles* Peggy Gray, *Costumes* Adele Palmer, Robert Ramsey, *Sound effects* Mandine Rogne, *Location manager* John T. Bourke, *Casting* Jack Grant, *Optical effects* Consolidated Film Industries. Copyright 12 April 1949 (chapters 1–6) and 9 May 1949 (chapters 7–12) by Republic Pictures Corporation; applied author: Republic Productions, Inc. RCA Photophone recording. Chapter 1, 20 minutes; all other chapters, 13 minutes each.

    Chapter titles: 1–Bandit Territory. 2–Forged Orders. 3–Robber's Agent. 4–Victims of Vengeance. 5–Gun Trap. 6–Deadline at Midnight. 7–Tower of Disaster. 8–Mob Justice. 9–Money Lure. 10–Message of Death. 11–Runaway Stagecoach. 12–Trail of Blood.

    Released in a 69-minute feature version, *Ghost of Zorro*, in 1959.

    Cast: *Ken Mason/Zorro* Clayton Moore, *Rita White* Pamela Blake, *Hank Kilgore* Roy Barcroft, *Moccasin* George J. Lewis, *George Crane* Eugene [Gene] Roth, *Mulvaney* John Crawford, *Paul Hobson* I. Stanford Jolley, *Jonathan R. White* Steve Clark, *Marshal Ben Simpson* Steve Darrell,

Mike Hodge/Mead Dale Van Sickel, *Brace/Spike* Tom Steele, *Yellow Hawk* Alex Montoya, *Fowler* Marshall Reed, *Doctor* Frank O'Connor, *Freight agent* Jack O'Shea, *Larkin* Holly Bane, *Andy* Bob Reeves, *Winch operator* Bob Robinson, *Black* John Daheim, *Morley* Kenneth Terrell, *Jim Cleaver* Edwin Parker, *Mike* Roger Creed, *Zeke/wagon driver* Post Parks, *Joe* Charles L. King, *Dan Foster* Stanley Blystone, *Jason* George Chesebro, *Indian dynamiter* Joseph Yrigoyen, *Townsman* Robert J. Wilke, *Townsman* Roy Bucko, *Townsman* Art Dillard, *Townsman* Frank Ellis.

Note: Clayton Moore became famous for later portraying another "Masked Avenger of the Plains."

King of the Rocket Men
(7 June 1949)

Credits: *Executive producer* Herbert J. Yates, *Producer* Franklyn Adreon, *Director* Fred C. Brannon, *Writers* Royal K. Cole, William Lively, Sol Shor, *Cinematography* Ellis W. Carter, *Process cinematography* Ellis J. Thackery, *Musical score* Stanley Wilson, *Musical director* Morton Scott, *Special effects* Howard Lydecker, Theodore Lydecker, *Production manager* John E. Baker, *Unit manager* Roy Wade, *Art direction* Ralph Oberg, Fred A. Ritter, *Set decorations* John McCarthy, Jr., James S. Redd, *Supervising editor* Murray Seldeen, *Editors* Clifford Bell, Sr., Sam Starr, *Sound* Earl Crain, Sr., Waldon O. Watson, *Makeup supervision* Robert Mark, *Hair styles* Peggy Gray, *Costumes* Adele Palmer, Robert Ramsey, *Sound effects* Mandine Rogne, *Location manager* John T. Bourke, *Casting* Jack Grant, *Optical effects* Consolidated Film Industries, Copyright 7 June 1949 (chapter 1), 19 July 1949 (chapters 2–7) and 17 August 1949 (chapters 8–12) by Republic Pictures Corporation; applied author: Republic Productions, Inc. RCA Photophone recording. Chapter 1, 20 minutes; all other chapters, 13 minutes each.

Chapter titles: 1–Dr. Vulcan — Traitor. 2–Plunging Death. 3–Dangerous Evidence. 4–High Peril. 5–Fatal Dive. 6–Mystery of the Rocket Man. 7–Molten Menace. 8–Suicide Flight. 9–Ten Seconds to Live. 10–The Deadly Fog. 11–Secret of Dr. Vulcan. 12–Wave of Disaster.

Released in a 65-minute feature version, *Lost Planet Airmen*, in 1951.

Cast: *Jeff King* Tristram Coffin, *Glenda Thomas* Mae Clark, *Tony Dirken* Don Haggerty, *Burt Winslow* House Peters, Jr., *Professor Millard* James Craven, *Professor Bryant/Dr. Vulcan* I. Stanford Jolley, *Chairman* Douglas Evans, *Martin Conway* Theodore Adams, *Gunther von Strum* Stanley Price, *Martin/Drake/Gates/Rand/Miller* Dale Van Sickel, *Knox/taxi driver/Chase* Tom Steele, *Blears/Cliff/Stark* David Sharpe, *Rowan* Edwin Parker, *Turk* Michael Ferro, *Guard* Frank O'Connor, *Phillips* Buddy Roosevelt, *Aide* Arvon Dale, *Clay* Bud Wolfe, *Graffner* Marshall Bradford,

An ad for *King of the Rocket Men* (1949). This serial and its sequels inspired the comic books which were the source for Disney's *The Rocketeer* (1991).

Morgan Bert LeBaron, *Newscaster* Art Gilmore, *Sparks* Carey Loftin, *Walter* Jack O'Shea.

Note: Sequels were *Radar Men from the Moon* (1952), *Zombies of the Stratosphere* (1952) and *Commando Cody, Sky Marshal of the Universe* (1953).

The James Brothers of Missouri
(4 October 1949)

Credits: *Executive producer* Herbert J. Yates, *Producer* Franklyn Adreon, *Director* Fred C. Brannon, *Writers* Royal K. Cole, William Lively, Sol Shor, *Cinematography* Ellis W. Carter, *Process cinematography* Ellis J. Thackery, *Musical score* Stanley Wilson, *Musical director* Morton Scott, *Special effects* Howard Lydecker, Theodore Lydecker, *Production manager* John E. Baker, *Unit manager* Roy Wade, *Art direction* Ralph Oberg, Fred A. Ritter, *Set decorations* John McCarthy, Jr., James S. Redd, *Supervising editor* Murray Seldeen, *Editors* Clifford Bell, Sr., Sam Starr, *Makeup supervision* Robert Mark, *Hair styles* Peggy Gray, *Costumes* Adele Palmer, Robert Ramsey, *Sound effects* Mandine Rogne, *Sound* Earl Crain, Sr., Waldon O. Watson, *Location manager* John T. Bourke, *Casting* Jack Grant, *Optical effects* Consolidated Film Industries. Copyright 4 October 1949 (chapters 1–6) and 28 October 1949 (chapters 7–12) by Republic Pictures Corporation; applied author: Republic Productions, Inc. RCA Photophone recording. Chapter 1, 20 minutes; all other chapters, 13 minutes each.

Chapter titles: 1–Frontier Renegades. 2–Racing Peril. 3–Danger Road. 4–Murder at Midnight. 5–Road to Oblivion. 6–Missouri Manhunt. 7–Hangman's Noose. 8–Coffin on Wheels. 9–Dead Man's Return. 10–Galloping Gunslingers. 11–The Haunting Past. 12–Fugitive Code.

Cast: *Jesse James* Keith Richards, *Frank James* Robert Bice, *Peggy*

Keith Richards and Robert Bice in *The James Brothers of Missouri* (1949).

Royer Noel Neill, *Ace Marlin* Roy Barcroft, *Belle Calhoun* Patricia Knox, *Monk Tucker* Lane Bradford, *Marshal Rand* Eugene [Gene] Roth, *Lon Royer* John Hamilton, *Sheriff* Edmund Cobb, *Duffy/Waller* Hank Patterson, *Simpson/Harry Sharkey* Dale Van Sickel, *Slim/Drake* Tom Steele, *Brandy Jones* Lee Roberts, *Townsman* Frank O'Connor, *Townsman* Robert J. Wilke, *Ed Thorne* Ted Hubert, *Dutch* Marshall Reed, *Stark/Trent* Kenneth Terrell, *Deputy sheriff* Wade Ray, *Price* Bert LeBaron, *Townsman/Knox* Tommy Coats, *Pop Keever* Nolan Leery, *Jackson* Joe Phillips, *Thug* Cactus Mack, *Bailey* David Sharpe, *Townsman/ Blears* Art Dillard, *Thug* Al Ferguson, *Cowl/Brad* Duke Green, *Pete/Flint* Fenton "Duke" Taylor, *Carson* John Crawford, *Wagon driver/Farrow* Post Parks, *Davis* Jim Rinehart, *Townsman/wagon driver* Ray Morgan, *Woman* Helen Griffith, *Man* Ralph Bucko, *Man* Rocky Shahan, *Man* Roy Bucko, *Man* Frosty Royce, *Man* Forrest Burns, *Man* Bud Wolfe, *Man* Charles Roberson, *Man* Herman Hack, *Man* Chick Hannon.

Radar Patrol vs. Spy King
(January 1950)

Credits: *Executive producer* Herbert J. Yates, *Producer* Franklyn Adreon, *Director* Fred C. Brannon, *Writers* Royal K. Cole, William Lively, Sol Shor, *Cinematography* Ellis W. Carter, *Process cinematography* Ellis J. Thackery, *Musical score* Stanley Wilson, *Musical director* Morton Scott, *Special effects* Howard Lydecker, Theodore Lydecker, *Production manager* John E. Baker, *Unit manager* Roy Wade, *Art direction* Ralph Oberg, Fred A. Ritter, *Set decorations* John McCarthy, Jr., Charles Thompson, *Supervising editor* Murray Seldeen, *Editors* Clifford Bell, Sr., Sam Starr, *Sound* Earl Crain, Sr., Waldon O. Watson, *Makeup supervision* Robert Mark, *Hair styles* Peggy Gray, *Costumes* Adele Palmer, Robert Ramsey, *Sound effects* Mandine Rogne, *Location manager* John T. Bourke, *Casting* Jack Grant, *Optical effects* Consolidated Film Industries. Copyright 28 December 1949 (chapters 1–6) and 14 February 1950 (chapters 7–12) by Republic Pictures Corporation; applied author: Republic Productions, Inc. RCA Photophone recording. Chapter 1, 20 minutes; all other chapters, 13 minutes each.

Chapter titles: 1–The Fatal Fog. 2–Perilous Trail. 3–Rolling Fury. 4–Flight of the Spy King. 5–Trapped Underground. 6–Wheels of Disaster. 7–Electrocution. 8–Death Rings the Phone. 9–Tomb of Terror. 10–Death Dive. 11–Desperate Mission. 12–Day of Reckoning.

Cast: *Chris Calvert* Kirk Alyn, *Joan Hughes* Jean Dean, *Ricco Morgan* Anthony Warde, *Manuel Agura* George J. Lewis, *Nitra* Eve Whitney, *John Baroda/The Spy King* John Merton, *Franklyn Lord* Tristram Coffin, *Sands* John Crawford, *Miller* Harold Goodwin, *Lentz/Thomas* Dale Van Sickel, *Ames/Gorman* Tom Steele, *Dutch/Bender/Herb/Nash/Malloy/White*

Eve Whitney and Kirk Alyn in *Radar Patrol vs. Spy King* (1950).

Edwin Parker, *Chairman* Forbes Murray, *Trooper* Arvan Dale, *Hugo* Stephen Gregory, *Tami* Kenneth Terrell, *John Clark* Frank Dae, *Nick* Bert LeBaron, *Police dispatcher* Roy Barcroft, *Link* Fenton "Duke" Taylor, *Cave henchman* Carey Loftin, *Kraft* Bud Wolfe, *Cliff* David Sharpe, *Jackson/ Hanley* John Daheim, *Finney* Charles Flynn, *Chairman* Frank O'Connor, *Man* Art Dillard, *Man* Buddy Joe Hooker, *Woman* Helen Thurston, *Woman* Louise Volding.

The Invisible Monster

(8 June 1950)

Credits: *Executive producer* Herbert J. Yates, *Producer* Franklyn Adreon, *Director* Fred C. Brannon, *Writer* Ronald Davidson, *Cinematography* Ellis W. Carter, *Process cinematography* Ellis J. Thackery, *Musical score* Stanley Wilson, *Musical director* Gerald Roberts, *Special effects* Howard Lydecker, Theodore Lydecker, *Production supervisor* John E. Baker, *Production manager* Lewis T. Rosso, *Unit manager* Roy Wade, *Art direction* Ralph Oberg, Fred A. Ritter, *Set decorations* John McCarthy, Jr., James S. Redd, *Supervising editor* Murray Seldeen, *Editors* Clifford Bell, Sr., Sam Starr, *Sound* Earl Crain, Sr., Waldon O. Watson, *Makeup supervision* Robert Mark, *Hair styles* Peggy Gray, *Costumes* Adele Palmer, Robert

Stanley Price in *The Invisible Monster* (1950).

Ramsey, *Dog trainer* Earl Johnson, *Location manager* John T. Bourke, *Casting* Jack Grant, *Optical effects* Consolidated Film Industries. Copyright 8 June 1950 (chapters 1–6) and 24 August 1950 (chapters 7–12) by Republic Pictures Corporation. RCA Photophone recording. Chapter 1, 20 minutes; all other chapters, 13 minutes each.

Chapter titles: 1–Slaves of the Phantom. 2–The Acid Clue. 3–The Death Car. 4–Highway Holocaust. 5–Bridge to Eternity. 6–Ordeal by Fire. 7–Murder Train. 8–Window of Peril. 9–Trail to Destruction. 10–High Voltage Danger. 11–Death's Highway. 12–The Phantom Meets Justice.

Released in a 100-minute feature version, *Slaves of the Invisible Monster*, in 1966.

Cast: *Lane Carson* Richard Webb, *Carol Richards* Aline Towne, *Burton* Lane Bradford, *The Phantom Ruler* Stanley Price, *Harris* John Crawford, *Harry Long* George Meeker, *Doctor* Keith Richards, *Martin/Otto Wagner* Dale Van Sickel, *Bill Haines/Mack* Tom Steele, *Policeman/McDuff* Marshall Reed, *Joe* Forrest Burns, *Stoner* Edwin Parker, *Hogan* Frank O'Connor, *Art/Al* Guy Teague, *Grogarty* Charles Sullivan, *Night watchman* Howard Mitchell, *Night watchman* Mark Strong, *Night* *watchman* Bert LeBaron, *Guard/night watchman* David Sharpe, *Harding* Bud Wolfe, *Guard* George Volk, *Dirk* Carey Loftin, *Gates* Tom Monroe, *James Hunter* Douglas Evans, *Kern* Kenneth Terrell, *Kirk* Harold Goodwin, *Warren Madison* Edward Keene, *Henry Miller* John Hamilton, *Moore* Roy Gordon, *Policeman* Fenton "Duke" Taylor, *Sam* George Magrill.

Desperadoes of the West
(17 August 1950)

Credits: *Executive producer* Herbert J. Yates, *Producer* Franklyn Adreon, *Director* Fred C. Brannon, *Writer* Ronald Davidson, *Cinematography* John MacBurnie, *Process cinematography* Ellis J. Thackery, *Musical score* Stanley Wilson, *Musical director* Gerald Roberts, *Special effects* Howard Lydecker, Theodore Lydecker, *Production supervisor* John E.

Richard Powers and Stanford Jolley in *Desperadoes of the West* (1950).

Baker, *Production manager* Lewis T. Rosso, *Unit manager* Roy Wade, *Art direction* Ralph Oberg, Fred A. Ritter, *Set decorations* John A. McCarthy, Jr., James S. Redd, *Supervising editor* Murray Seldeen, *Editors* Clifford Bell, Sr., Sam Starr, *Makeup supervision* Robert Mark, *Hair styles* Peggy Gray, *Sound* Richard Tyler, Waldon O. Watson, *Costumes* Adele Palmer, Robert Ramsey, *Location manager* John T. Bourke, *Casting* Jack Grant, *Optical effects* Consolidated Film Industries. Copyright 17 August 1950 (chapters 1–3 and preview trailer) and 12 October 1950 (chapters 4–12) by Republic Pictures Corporation; applied author: Republic Productions, Inc. RCA Photophone recording. Chapter 1, 20 minutes; all other chapters, 13 minutes each.

    Chapter titles: 1–Tower of Jeopardy. 2–Perilous Barrier. 3–Flaming Cargo. 4–Trail of Terror. 5–Plunder Cave. 6–Six-Gun Hijacker. 7–The Powder Keg. 8–Desperate Venture. 9–Stagecoach to Eternity. 10–Hidden Desperado. 11–Open Warfare. 12–Desperate Gamble.

    Cast: *Ward Gordon* Richard Powers, *Sally Arnold* Judy Clark, *Hacker* Roy Barcroft, *J. B. Dawson* I. Stanford Jolley, *Rusty Steele* Lee Phelps, *Larson* Lee Roberts, *Colonel Arnold* Cliff Clark, *Bowers* Edmund Cobb, *Hard Rock Haggerty* Hank Patterson, *Reed* Dale Van Sickel, *Gregg/Blake* Tom Steele, *Kern* Sandy Sanders, *Casey* John Cason, *Jack* Guy Teague, *Joe* Bud Osborne, *Storekeeper* Stanley Blystone, *Al* Charles Hayward, *Tom* Forrest Burns, *Bert* Bert LeBaron, *Todd* Jack Ingram, *Barkeeper* Frank O'Connor, *Sheriff* Harold Goodwin, *Becker* George Chesebro, *Rock* Ralph Bucko, *Ben* Art Dillard, *Plummer* Fred Kohler, Jr., *Bryant* Holly Bane, *Oil worker* Paul Gustine, *Cody* Fenton "Duke" Taylor, *Bill Murdock* John Daheim, *Drake* Cactus Mack, *Martin* Edwin Parker, *Ed* Ken Cooper, *Larkin* Tom McDonough, *Ned Foster* Dennis Moore, *Jerry* Bob Reeves, *Freight agent* Steve Clark, *Jensen* Al Taylor, *Guard* Chick Hannon, *Horseman* Ace Hudkins, *Hadley* Mauritz Hugo, *Ed Harper* Jack Harden, *Citizen* Jim Rinehart, *Citizen* Billy Dix, *Citizen* Ray Morgan, *Man* Wayne Burson, *Man* Augie Gomez, *Man* Merrill McCormick, *Man* Joe Phillips.

Flying Disc Man from Mars
(December 1950)

    Credits: *Executive producer* Herbert J. Yates, *Producer* Franklyn Adreon, *Director* Fred C. Brannon, *Writer* Ronald Davidson, *Cinematography* Walter Strenge, *Process cinematography* Ellis J. Thackery, *Musical score* Stanley Wilson, *Musical director* Gerald Roberts, *Special effects* Howard Lydecker, Theodore Lydecker, *Production supervisor* John E. Baker, *Production manager* Lewis T. Rosso. *Unit manager* Roy Wade, *Art direction* Ralph Oberg, Fred A. Ritter, *Set decorations* John McCarthy, Jr., James S. Redd, *Supervising editor* Murray Seldeen, *Editors* Clifford Bell, Sr., Sam Starr, *Sound* Earl Crain, Sr., Waldon O. Watson, *Makeup*

Harry Lauter (second from right) and henchmen in *Flying Disc Man from Mars* (1950).

supervision Robert Mark, *Hair styles* Peggy Gray, *Costumes* Adele Palmer, Robert Ramsey, *Location manager* John T. Bourke, *Casting* Jack Grant, *Optical effects* Consolidated Film Industries. Copyright 30 November 1950 (chapters 1–3) and 21 December 1950 (chapters 4–12) by Republic Pictures Corporation. RCA Photophone recording. Chapter 1, 20 minutes; all other chapters, 13 minutes each.

Chapter titles: 1–Menace from Mars. 2–The Volcano's Secret. 3–Death Rides the Stratosphere. 4–Execution by Fire. 5–The Living Projectile. 6–Perilous Mission. 7–Descending Doom. 8–Suicidal Sacrifice. 9–The Funeral Pyre. 10–Weapons of Hate. 11–Disaster on the Highway. 12–Volcanic Vengeance.

Released in a 75-minute feature version, *Missile Monsters*, on 12 November 1958.

Cast: *Kent Fowler* Walter Reed, *Helen Hall* Lois Collier, *Mota* Gregory Gay, *Dr. Bryant* James Craven, *Drake* Harry Lauter, *Ryan* Richard Irving, *Steve* Sandy Sanders, *Trent* Michael Carr, *Watchman* Dale Van Sickel, *Taylor* Tom Steele, *Gateman* George Sherwood, *Grady* Jimmy O'Gatty, *Curtis* John DeSimmons, *Crane* Lester Dorr, *Kirk* Richard Cogan, *Lewis Ashe* Clayton Moore, *Bill* Richard Crockett, *Boyd* John Daheim, *Cole* Bill Wilkus, *Driver* Chuck Hamilton, *Ed* Saul Gorss, *Garrett*

Barry Brooks, *Graves* Kenneth Terrell, *Hagen* Carey Loftin, *Technician* David Sharpe, *Technician* Paul Gustine, *Workman* Guy Teague.

Don Daredevil Rides Again
(23 May 1951)

Credits: *Executive producer* Herbert J. Yates, *Producer* Franklyn Adreon, *Director* Fred C. Brannon, *Writer* Ronald Davidson, *Cinematography* Ellis W. Carter, *Musical score* Stanley Wilson, *Musical director* Gerald Roberts, *Special effects* Howard Lydecker, Theodore Lydecker, *Production supervisor* John E. Baker, *Production manager* Lewis T. Rosso, *Unit manager* Roy Wade, *Art direction* Ralph Oberg, Fred A. Ritter, *Set decorations* John McCarthy, Jr., Charles Thompson, *Supervising editor* Murray Seldeen, *Editor* Clifford Bell, Sr., *Sound* Earl Crain, Sr., Waldon O. Watson, *Makeup supervision* Robert Mark, *Hair styles* Peggy Gray, *Costumes* Adele Palmer, Robert Ramsey, *Location manager* John T. Bourke, *Casting* Jack Grant, *Process cinematography* Ellis J. Thackery, *Optical effects* Consolidated Film Industries. Copyright 23 May 1951 (chapters 1–4 and preview trailer) and 7 June 1951 (chapters 5–12) by Republic Pictures Corporation; applied author: Republic Productions, Inc. RCA Photophone recording. Chapter 1, 20 minutes; all other chapters, 13 minutes each.

An ad for *Don Daredevil Rides Again* (1951).

Chapter titles: 1–Return of the Don. 2–Double Death. 3–Hidden Danger. 4–Retreat to Destruction. 5–Cold Steel. 6–The Flaming Juggernaut. 7–Claim Jumper. 8–Perilous Combat. 9–Hostage of Destiny. 10–Marked for Murder. 11–The Captive Witness. 12–Flames of Vengeance.

Cast: *Lee Hadley/Don Daredevil* Ken Curtis, *Patricia Doyle* Aline Towne, *Douglas Stration* Roy Barcroft, *Weber* Lane Bradford, *Gary Taylor* Robert Einer, *Hagen* John Cason, *Sheriff* I. Stanford Jolley, *Buck Bender* Hank Patterson, *Uncle Michael* Lee Phelps, *Dirk* Sandy Sanders, *Deputy sheriff* Guy Teague, *Deputy sheriff* Frank McCarroll, *Black* Tom Steele, *Miller* Cactus Mack, *Attacker/raider* Art Dillard, *Attacker* Joe Phillips, *Barnett* Roy Bucko, *Bartender* Bud Osborne, *Briggs* Saul Gorss, *Caleb Brown* Gene Stutenroth [Gene Roth], *Carson* James Magrill, *Clark* David Sharpe, *Davis* Charles Horvath, *Dan Farley* Dale Van Sickel, *Jack* Jack Ingram, *Martin* George Lloyd, *Jake Miller* Jack Harden, *Owens* Carey Loftin, *Sloan* Carlie Taylor, *Taylor* Forrest Taylor, *Tex* Bert LeBaron, *Thompson* James Linn, *Citizen* Gene Christopher, *Citizen* Tony DeMario, *Citizen* Don C. Harvey, *Citizen* Frank Meredith, *Citizen* Tex Terry, *Citizen* Bob Reeves, *Citizen* Chick Hannon, *Citizen* Herman Hack.

Government Agents vs. Phantom Legion
(23 August 1951)

Credits: *Executive producer:* Herbert J. Yates, *Producer* Franklyn Adreon, *Director* Fred C. Brannon, *Writer* Ronald Davidson, *Cinematography* John L. Russell, Jr., *Musical score* Stanley Wilson, *Musical director*

An ad for *Government Agents vs. Phantom Legion* (1951).

Richard Curtis and Walter Reed in *Government Agents vs. Phantom Legion* (1951).

Gerald Roberts, *Special effects* Howard Lydecker, Theodore Lydecker, *Art director* Ralph Oberg, Fred A. Ritter, *Set decorations* John McCarthy, Jr., James S. Redd, *Production supervisor* John E. Baker, *Production manager* Lewis T. Rosso, *Unit manager* Roy Wade, *Supervising editor* Murray Seldeen, *Editor* Clifford Bell, Sr., *Sound* Earl Crain, Sr., Waldon O. Watson, *Costumes* Adele Palmer, Robert Ramsey, *Makeup supervision* Robert Mark. *Hair styles* Peggy Gray, *Location manager* John T. Bourke, *Casting* Jack Grant, *Process cinematography* Ellis J. Thackery, *Optical effects* Consolidated Film Industries. Copyright 23 August 1951 (all chapters) by Republic Pictures Corporation; applied author: Republic Productions, Inc. RCA Photophone recording. Chapter 1, 20 minutes; all other chapters, 13 minutes each.

    Chapter titles: 1–River of Fire. 2–The Stolen Corpse. 3–The Death Drop. 4–Doorway to Doom. 5–Deadline for Disaster. 6–Mechanical Homicide. 7–The Flaming Highway. 8–Sea Saboteurs. 9–Peril Underground. 10–Execution by Accident. 11–Perilous Plunge. 12–Blazing Retribution.

    Cast: *Hal Duncan* Walter Reed, *Kay Roberts* Mary Ellen Kay, *Regan* Richard Curtis, *Sam Bradley* John Pickard, *Cady* Fred Cody, *Armstrong/ The Voice* Pierce Lyden, *Willard* George Meeker, *J. J. Patterson* John Phillips, *Thompson* Mauritz Hugo, *Turner* Edmund Cobb, *Barnett* Eddie Dew,

Coroner George Lloyd, *Brice/Kern* Dale Van Sickel, *Brandt* Tom Steele, *Crandall* Arthur Space, *District attorney* Norval Mitchell, *Motorcycle patrolman* Frank Meredith, *Bystander* Gene Christopher, *Car thug* Terry Frost, *Casey* Frank Alten, *Crane* Richard Crockett, *Daly* George Volk, *Dispatcher* Roy Barcroft, *Donovan* Ben Taggart, *Gas station attendant* Richard Grant, *Gray* Dean Henson, *Hospital orderly* Jay Merrick, *Kirk* Fenton "Duke" Taylor, *Larson* Buddy Thorpe, *McGee* Ralph Dunn, *Miller* Joe Phillips, *Payne* Edwin Parker, *Policeman* Frank O'Connor, *Man* David Sharpe.

Radar Men from the Moon
(9 January 1952)

Credits: *Executive producer* Herbert J. Yates, *Producer* Franklyn Adreon, *Director* Fred C. Brannon, *Screenplay* Ronald Davidson, *Based on characters created by* Royal K. Cole, William Lively, Sol Shor, *Cinematography* John MacBurnie, *Musical score* Stanley Wilson, *Musical director* Gerald Roberts, *Special effects* Howard Lydecker, Theodore Lydecker, *Production supervisor* John E. Baker, *Production manager* Lewis T. Rosso, *Unit manager* Roy Wade, *Art direction* Ralph Oberg, Fred A. Ritter, *Set decorations* John McCarthy, Jr., James S. Redd, *Sound* Richard Tyler, Waldon O. Watson, *Makeup supervision* Robert Mark, *Hair styles* Peggy Gray, *Supervising editor* Murray Seldeen, *Editor* Clifford Bell, Sr., *Costumes* Adele Palmer, Robert Ramsey, *Location manager* John T. Bourke, *Casting* Jack Grant, *Process cinematography* Ellis J. Thackery, *Optical effects* Consolidated Film Industries. Copyright 9 January 1952 (in notice 1951; chapters 1–6 and preview trailer) and 3 January 1952 (in notice 1951; chapters 7–12) by Republic Pictures Corporation. RCA Photophone recording. Chapter 1, 20 minutes; all other chapters, 13 minutes each.

Chapter titles: 1–Moon Rocket. 2–Molten Terror. 3–Bridge of Death. 4–Flight to Destruction. 5–Murder Car. 6–Hills of Death. 7–Human Targets. 8–The Enemy Planet. 9–Battle in the Stratosphere. 10–Mass Execution. 11–Planned Pursuit. 12–Take-Off to Eternity.

Released in a 100-minute feature version, *Retik the Moon Menace*, in 1966.

Cast: *Commando Cody* George Wallace, *Joan Gilbert* Aline Towne, *Retik* Roy Barcroft, *Ted Richards* William Bakewell, *Graber* Clayton Moore, *Krog* Peter Brocco, *Daly* Bob Stevenson, *Henderson* Don Walters, *Zerg* Tom Steele, *Alon* Dale Van Sickel, *Hank* Wilson Wood, *Robal* Noel Cravat, *Nasor* Baynes Barron, *Bream* Robert McGuire, *Bartender* Ted Thorpe, *Jones* Dick Cogan, *Benson* Stephen Gregory, *Bill* Paul Palmer, *Brad* Henry Hollins, *Citizen* Carey Loftin, *Doyle* Jack O'Shea, *Duke* Billy Dix, *Guard* William Marke, *Kern* Claude Dunkin, *Moon Scout 7* Sam Sebby, *Motorcycle patrolman* Arthur Walsh, *Policeman* Joe Bailey, *Policeman*

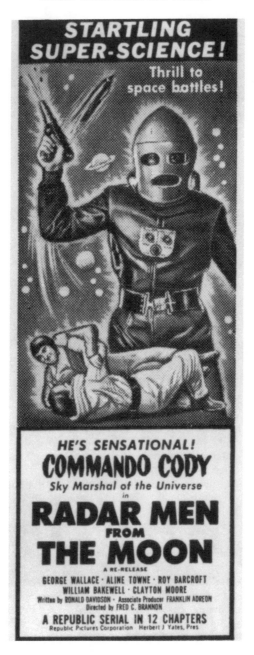

A reissue ad for *Radar Men from the Moon* (1952).

Guy Teague, *Policeman* Dick Rich, *Sam* Tony Merrill, *Smith* John Marshall, *Man* Kenneth Terrell.

Zombies of the Stratosphere
(16 July 1952)

Credits: *Executive producer* Herbert J. Yates, *Producer* Franklyn Adreon, *Director* Fred C. Brannon, *Screenplay* Ronald Davidson, *Based on characters created by* Royal K. Cole, William Lively, Sol Shor, *Cinematography* John MacBurnie, *Musical score* Stanley Wilson, *Musical director* Gerald Roberts, *Special effects* Howard Lydecker, Theodore Lydecker, *Production supervisor* John E. Baker, *Production manager* Lewis T. Rosso, *Unit manager* Roy Wade, *Art direction* Ralph Oberg, Fred A. Ritter, *Set decorations* John McCarthy, Jr., James S. Redd, *Supervising editor* Murray Seldeen, *Editor* Clifford Bell, Sr., *Sound* Richard Tyler, Waldon O. Watson, *Makeup supervision* Robert Mark, *Hair styles* Peggy Gray, *Costumes* Adele Palmer, Alec Davidoff, *Location manager* John T. Bourke, *Casting* Jack Grant, *Process cinematography* Ellis J. Thackery, *Optical effects* Consolidated Film Industries. Copyright 2 July 1952 (all chapters and preview trailer) by Republic Pictures Corporation. RCA Photophone recording. Chapter 1, 20 minutes; all other chapters, 13 minutes each.

From left, Aline Towne, Judd Holdren, Wilson Wood and robot in *Zombies of the Stratosphere* (1952). Republic's prop shop originally built the robot suit for *Undersea Kingdom* and it was employed thereafter anytime the studio needed a mechanical menace. It eventually appeared in several chapterplays into the fifties.

Chapter titles: 1–The Zombie Vanguard. 2–Battle of the Rockets. 3–Undersea Agents. 4–Contraband Cargo. 5–The Iron Executioner. 6–Murder Mine. 7–Death on the Waterfront. 8–Hostage for Murder. 9–The Human Torpedo. 10–Flying Gas Chamber. 11–Man vs. Monster. 12–Tomb of the Traitors.

ColorImaged by American Film Technologies in 1990. Released in a 70-minute feature version, *Satan's Satellites*, on 12 May 1958.

Cast: *Larry Martin* Judd Holdren, *Sue Davis* Aline Towne, *Bob Wilson* Wilson Wood, *Marex* Lane Bradford, *Dr. Harding* Stanley Waxman, *Roth* John Crawford, *Mr. Steele* Craig Kelly, *Shane* Ray Boyle, *Narab* Leonard Nimoy, *Truck driver/Walker* Tom Steele, *Telegrapher* Dale Van Sickel, *Lawson* Roy Engel, *Kerr* Jack Harden, *Fisherman* Paul Stader, Sr., *Dick* Gayle Kellogg, *Policeman* Jack Shea, *Policeman* Floyd Criswell, *Policeman* Davison Clark, *Elah* Robert Garabedian, *Gomez operator* Jack Mack, *Kettler* Robert Strange, *Pilot* Paul Gustine, *Plane thug* Henry Rowland, *Ross* Clifton Young, *Tarner* Norman Willis, *Train thug* George Magrill, *Train thug* Frank Alten, *Man* John Daheim, *Man* Kenneth Terrell, *Voices* Roy Barcroft.

Jungle Drums of Africa
(19 December 1952)

Credits: *Executive producer* Herbert J. Yates, *Producer* Franklyn Adreon, *Director* Fred C. Brannon, *Writer* Ronald Davidson, *Cinematography* John MacBurnie, *Musical score* Stanley Wilson, *Musical director* Gerald Roberts, *Special effects* Howard Lydecker, Theodore Lydecker, *Production supervisor* John E. Baker, *Production manager* Lewis T. Rosso, *Unit manager* Roy Wade, *Art direction* Ralph Oberg, Fred A. Ritter, *Set decorations* John McCarthy, Jr., George Milo, *Supervising editor* Murray Seldeen, *Editors* Clifford Bell, Sr., Joseph Harrison, *Sound* Thomas A. Carman, Waldon O. Watson, *Makeup supervision* Robert Mark, *Hair styles* Peggy Gray, *Costumes* Adele Palmer, Alec Davidoff, *Chiquita's owner and trainer* Jack "Pinky" Jackson, *Location manager* John T. Bourke, *Casting* Jack Grant, *Process cinematography* Ellis J. Thackery, *Optical effects* Consolidated Film Industries. Copyright 19 December 1952 (all chapters and preview trailer) by Republic Pictures Corporation. RCA Photophone recording. Chapter 1, 20 minutes; all other chapters, 13 minutes each.

Chapter titles: 1–Jungle Ambush. 2–Savage Strategy. 3–The Beast-Fiend. 4–Voodoo Vengeance. 5–The Lion Pit. 6–Underground Tornado. 7–Cavern of Doom. 8–The Water Trap. 9–Trail of Destruction. 10–The Flaming Ring. 11–Bridge of Death. 12–The Avenging River.

Released in a 100-minute feature version, *U-238 and the Witch Doctor*, in 1966.

Cast: *Alan King* Clayton Moore, *Carol Bryant* Phyllis Coates, *Bert*

From front left, Clayton Moore, Roy Glenn, Sr., Phyllis Coates, Johnny Spencer and natives in *Jungle Drums of Africa* (1952).

Hadley Johnny Spencer, *Naganto* Roy Glenn, Sr., *Regas* John Cason, Kurgan Henry Rowland, *Gauss* Steve Mitchell, *Chief Douanga* Bill Walker, *Ebola* Don Blackman, *Nodala* Felix Nelson, *Matambo* Joel Fluellen, *Tembo* Bill Washington, *First constable* Roy Engel, *Second constable* Tom Steele, *First native* Robert Davis, *Second native* Bob Johnson, *Nicky* Chiquita, *Man* DeForest Covan, *Man* Walter Smith, *Man* Maxie Thrower, *Man* Joseph Yrigoyen.

Commando Cody, Sky Marshal of the Universe
(17 February 1953)

Credits: *Executive producer* Herbert J. Yates, *Producer* Franklyn Adreon, *Directors* Fred C. Brannon, Harry Keller, Franklyn Adreon, *Screenplay* Ronald Davidson, Barry Shipman, *Based on characters created by* Ronald Davidson, Royal K. Cole, William Lively, Sol Shor, *Cinematography* Ellis J. Thackery, *Musical score* Stanley Wilson, *Musical director* Gerald Roberts, *Special effects* Howard Lydecker, Theodore Lydecker, *Production supervisor* John E. Baker, *Production manager* Lewis T. Rosso, *Unit manager* Roy Wade, *Art direction* Ralph Oberg, Frank Arrigo, *Set decorations* John McCarthy, Jr., *Makeup supervision* Robert Mark, *Hair styles* Peggy Gray, *Costumes* Adele Palmer, Alec Davidoff, *Supervising editor* Murray Seldeen, *Editors* Clifford Bell, Sr., Harold A. Minter, *Sound* Waldon O. Watson, *Location manager* John T. Bourke, *Casting* Jack Grant, *Optical effects* Consolidated Film Industries. Copyright 17 February 1953 (chapter 1), 27 February 1953 (chapters 2, 3), 18 May 1953 (chapter 4), 4 June 1953 (chapters 5–7; chapter 7 applied title *Robot Monster of Mars*), 6 July 1953 (chapter 8), 17 July 1953 (chapter 10), 23 July 1953 (chapter 11), 27 July 1953 (chapters 9–12) by Republic Pictures Corporation. RCA Photophone recording. All chapters, 27 minutes each.

Chapter titles: 1–Enemies of the Universe. 2–Atomic Peril. 3–Cosmic Vengeance. 4–Nightmare Typhoon. 5–War of the Space Giants. 6–Destroyers of the Sun. 7–Robot Monster from Mars. 8–Hydrogen Hurricane. 9–Solar Sky Riders. 10–S.O.S. Ice Age. 11–Lost in Outer Space. 12–Captives of the Zero Hour.

Cast: *Jeff King* Judd Holdren, *Joan Albright* Aline Towne, *Ted Richards* William Schallert, *Retik* Gregory Gay, *Dr. Varney* Peter Brocco, *Henderson* Craig Kelly, Lyle Talbot, *and* Dale Van Sickel.

Note: This was a most unusual chapterplay for the sound era, though a common format during the silent days. Made for television as a half hour series, each chapter was a story unto itself while at the same time having a definite continuity. It was released theatrically prior to its syndication and could be booked as a full 12-episode chapterplay or individual chapters could be exhibited as specialty short subjects. It was telecast over the National Broadcasting Company from 16 July 1955 to 8 October 1955. The title is usually given as *Commando Cody* rather than the full applied title above.

Canadian Mounties vs. Atomic Invaders
(8 June 1953)

Credits: *Executive producer* Herbert J. Yates, *Producer and director* Franklyn Adreon, *Writer* Ronald Davidson, *Cinematography* John MacBurnie, *Musical score* Stanley Wilson, *Musical director* Gerald Roberts, *Special effects* Howard Lydecker, Theodore Lydecker, *Assistant director* Arthur J. Vitarelli, *Production supervisor* John E. Baker, *Production manager* Lewis T. Rosso, *Unit manager* Roy Wade, *Art direction* Ralph Oberg, Fred A. Ritter, *Set decorations* John McCarthy, Jr., James S. Redd, *Sound* Richard Tyler, Waldon O. Watson, *Supervising editor* Murray Seldeen, *Editors* Clifford Bell, Sr., Joseph Harrison, *Makeup supervision* Robert Mark, *Hair styles* Peggy Gray, *Costumes* Adele Palmer, Alec Davidoff, *Location manager* John T. Bourke, *Casting* Jack Grant, *Process cinematography* Ellis J. Thackery, *Optical effects* Consolidated Film Industries. Copyright 8 June 1953 (all chapters and preview trailer) by

Dale Van Sickel and Bill Henry in *Canadian Mounties vs. Atomic Invaders* (1953).

Republic Pictures Corporation. RCA Photophone recording. Chapter 1, 20 minutes; all other chapters, 13 minutes each.

Chapter titles: 1–Arctic Intrigue. 2–Murder or Accident? 3–Fangs of Death. 4–Underground Inferno. 5–Pursuit to Destruction. 6–The Boat Trap. 7–Flame versus Gun. 8–Highway of Horror. 9–Doomed Cage. 10–Human Quarry. 11–Mechanical Homicide. 12–Cavern of Revenge.

Released in a 100-minute feature version, *Missile Base at Taniak*, in 1966.

Cast: *Sergeant Don Roberts* Bill Henry, *Kay Conway* Susan Morrow, *Marlof/Smokey Joe* Arthur Space, *Beck* Dale Van Sickel, *Commissioner Morrison* Pierre Watkin, *Reed* Mike Regan, *Anderson* Stanley Andrews, *Clark* Harry Lauter, *Jed Larson* Hank Patterson, *Mr. Warner* Edmund Cobb, *Corporal Guy Sanders* Gayle Kellogg, *Mack* Tom Steele, *Betty Warner* Jean Wright, *Mrs. Anderson* Jean Wood, *Bartender* Bob Reeves, *Launch thug* Joseph Yrigoyen, *Launch thug* Carey Loftin, *Mailman* Duane Thorsen, *Mason* Fred Graham, *Mills* Drew Cahill, *Murphy* William Fawcett, *Officer* Kenner Kemp, *Ed Olson* Gordon Armitage, *Ed Peters* George DeNormand, *Turner* Paul Palmer, *Man* Earl Bunn, *Man* James Fawcett, *Man* David Sharpe, *Man* Bob Jamison, *Man* Fenton "Duke" Taylor.

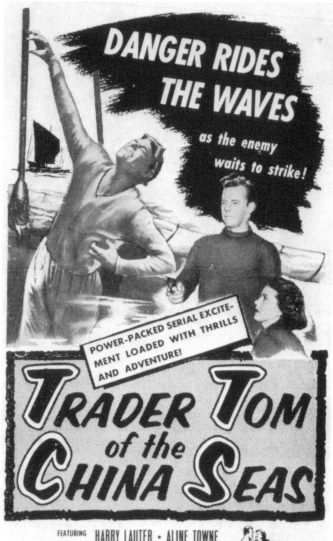

An ad for *Trader Tom of the China Seas* (1954).

Trader Tom of the China Seas
(6 January 1954)

Credits: *Executive producer* Herbert J. Yates, *Producer and director* Franklyn Adreon, *Writer* Ronald Davidson, *Cinematography* Ellis J. Thackery, *Musical score* R. Dale Butts, *Musical director* Gerald Roberts, *Special effects* Howard Lydecker, Theodore Lydecker, *Assistant director* Robert Shannon, *Production supervisor* John E. Baker, *Production manager* Lewis T. Rosso, *Unit manager* Roy Wade, *Art direction* Ralph Oberg, Frank Hotaling, *Set decorations* John McCarthy, Jr., Bertram Granger, *Sound* Earl Crain, Sr., Waldon O. Watson, *Supervising editor* Murray Seldeen, *Editor* Clifford Bell, Sr., *Makeup supervision* Robert Mark, *Hair styles* Peggy Gray, *Costumes* Adele Palmer, Alec Davidoff, *Location manager* John T. Bourke, *Casting* Jack Grant, *Optical effects* Consolidated Film Industries. Copyright 6 January 1954 (chapters 1–3 and preview trailer) and 13 January 1954 (chapters 4–12) by Republic Pictures Corporation. Vast Vision. RCA Photophone recording. Chapter 1, 20 minutes; all other chapters, 13 minutes each.

Chapter titles: 1–Sea Saboteurs. 2–Death Takes the Deck. 3–Five Fathoms Down. 4–On Target! 5–The Fire Ship. 6–Collision! 7–War in the Hills. 8–Native Execution. 9–Mass Attack. 10–Machine Murder. 11–Underwater Ambush. 12–Twisted Vengeance.

Released in a 100-minute feature version, *Target: Sea of China*, in 1966.

Cast: *Tom Rogers* Harry Lauter, *Vivian Wells* Aline Towne, *Barent* Lyle Talbot, *Major Conroy* Robert Shayne, *Kurt Daley* Fred Graham, *Rebel chief* Richard Reeves, *Gursan/Mike* Tom Steele, *Bill Gaines* John Crawford, *Native bushwacker* Dale Van Sickel, *Wang* Victor Sen Yung, *Khan* Jan Arvan, *British colonel* Ramsey Hill, *Ole* George Selk, *Baggage clerk* Charley Phillips, *James Dean* Bill Hudson, *Fireman/native* Bert LeBaron, *Gorth* Richard Alexander, *Hal* Duane Thorsen, *Mate* Kenneth Terrell, *Native* Saul Gorss, *Native horseman* Steve Conte, *Paine* Robert Bice, *Pilot* Charles Sullivan, *Soldier* William Chandler, *Train thug* Budd Buster, *Yank* Rush Williams, *Man* Jerry Brown.

Man with the Steel Whip
(19 July 1954)

Credits: *Executive producer* Herbert J. Yates, *Producer and director* Franklyn Adreon, *Writer* Ronald Davidson, *Cinematography* Ellis J. Thackery, *Musical score* R. Dale Butts, *Musical director* Gerald Roberts, *Special effects* Howard Lydecker, Theodore Lydecker, *Production super*

An ad for *Man with the Steel Whip* (1954).

visor John E. Baker, *Production manager* Lewis T. Rosso, *Unit manager* Roy Wade, *Assistant director* Arthur J. Vitarelli, *Art direction* Ralph Oberg, Frank Arrigo, *Set decorations* John McCarthy, Jr., George Milo, *Sound* Thomas A. Carman, Waldon O. Watson, *Supervising editor* Murray Seldeen, *Editors* Clifford Bell, Sr., Joseph Harrison, *Makeup supervision* Robert Mark, *Hair styles* Peggy Gray, *Costumes* Adele Palmer, Alec Davidoff, *Location manager* John T. Bourke, *Casting* Jack Grant, *Optical effects* Consolidated Film Industries. Copyright 19 July 1954 (all chapters and preview trailer) by Republic Pictures Corporation. VastVision. RCA Photophone recording. Chapter 1, 20 minutes; all other chapters, 13 minutes each.

    Chapter titles: 1–The Spirit Rider. 2–Savage Fury. 3–Mask of El Latigo. 4–The Murder Cave. 5–The Stone Guillotine. 6–Flame and Battle. 7–Double Ambush. 8–The Blazing Barrier. 9–The Silent Informer. 10–Window of Death. 11–The Fatal Masquerade. 12–Redskin Raiders.

    Cast: *Jerry Randall/El Latigo* Richard Simmons, *Nancy Cooper* Barbara Bestar, *Crane* Dale Van Sickel, *Barnett* Mauritz Hugo, *Tosco* Lane Bradford, *Indian chief* Pat Hogan, *Sheriff* Roy Barcroft, *Harris* Stuart Randall, *Lee* Edmund Cobb, *Sloane* I. Stanford Jolley, *Price* Guy Teague, *Quivar* Alan Wells, *Tom/Gage* Tom Steele, *Barn thug* Art Dillard, *Barn thug* Charles Hayward, *Blackjack Sam* Charles Stevens, *Harker* Jerry Brown, *Jim Kirkwood* Harry Harvey, *Mack* Robert Clarke, *Mike* Charles Sullivan, *Orca* Robert "Buzz" Henry, *Road worker* Tom Monroe, *Sam* Chris Mitchell, *Stanton* Gregg Barton, *Clem Stokes* George Eldredge, *Citizen* Tex Terry, *Citizen* Walter LaRue, *Citizen* Herman Hack.

Panther Girl of the Kongo
(3 January 1955)

    Credits: *Executive producer* Herbert J. Yates, *Producer and director* Franklyn Adreon, *Writer* Ronald Davidson, *Cinematography* Ellis J. Thackery, *Musical score* R. Dale Butts, *Musical director* Gerald Roberts, *Special effects* Howard Lydecker, Theodore Lydecker, *Production supervisor* John E. Baker, *Production manager* Lewis T. Rosso, *Unit manager* Roy Wade, *Assistant director* Leonard Kunody, *Art direction* Ralph Oberg, Frank Hotaling, *Set decorations* John McCarthy, Jr., Edward G. Boyle, *Supervising editor* Murray Seldeen, *Editor* Clifford Bell, Sr., *Sound* Roy Meadows, Waldon O. Watson, *Makeup supervision* Robert Mark, *Hair styles* Peggy Gray, *Costumes* Adele Palmer, Alec Davidoff, *Location manager* John T. Bourke, *Casting* Jack Grant, *Optical effects* Consolidated Film Industries. Copyright 3 January 1955 (in notice 1954) (all chapters and preview trailer) by Republic Pictures Corporation. VastVision. RCA

Phyllis Coates and Steve Calvert in *Panther Girl of the Kongo* (1955). The gorilla wasn't one of the Claw Monsters. They were gigantic crayfish enlarged by the villain.

Photophone recording. Chapter 1, 20 minutes; all other chapters, 13 minutes each.

Chapter titles: 1–The Claw Monster. 2–Jungle Ambush. 3–The Killer Beast. 4–Sands of Doom. 5–Test of Terror. 6–High Peril. 7–Timber Trap. 8–Crater of Flame. 9–River of Death. 10–Blasted Evidence. 11–Double Danger. 12–House of Doom.

Released in a 100-minute feature version, *The Claw Monsters*, in 1966.

Cast: *Jean Evans* Phyllis Coates, *Larry Sanders* Myron Healey, *Doctor Morgan* Arthur Space, *Cass* John Day [John Daheim], *Rand* Mike Regan, *Tembu* Morris Buchanan, *Chief Danka* Roy Glenn, Sr., *Ituri* Archie Savage, *Commissioner Stanton* Ramsay Hill, *Orto* Naaman Brown, *Ebu* Dan Ferniel, *Harris* James Logan, *Bartender* Gene Stutenroth [Gene Roth], *Nick Burgas* Fred Graham, *Davis* Charles Sullivan, *Gorilla* Steve Calvert, *Kent* Keith McConnell, *Koango* DeForest Covan, *Naganto* Walter Smith, *Native* Daniel Elam, *Native* Wesley Gale, *Semba* Don Carlos, *Stanley* Alan Reynolds, *Zemba* Martin Wilkins, *Man* Tom Steele.

King of the Carnival
(11 May 1955)

Credits: *Executive producer* Herbert J. Yates, *Producer and director* Franklyn Adreon, *Writer* Ronald Davidson, *Cinematography* Ellis J. Thackery, *Musical score* R. Dale Butts, *Musical director* Gerald Roberts, *Special effects* Howard Lydecker, Theodore Lydecker, *Assistant director* Leonard Kunody, *Production supervisor* John E. Baker, *Production manager* Lewis T. Rosso, *Unit manager* Roy Wade, *Art direction* Ralph Oberg, Fred A. Ritter, *Set decorations* John McCarthy, Jr., Otto Siegel, *Supervising editor* Murray Seldeen, *Editor* Joseph Harrison, *Sound* Hugh

An ad for *King of the Carnival* (1955).

Harry Lauter, Robert Shayne and spectators in *King of the Carnival* (1955).

McDowell, Jr., Waldon O. Watson, *Makeup and hair supervision* Robert Mark, *Costumes* Adele Palmer, Alec Davidoff, *Location manager* John T. Bourke, *Casting* Jack Grant, *Optical effects* Consolidated Film Industries. Copyright 11 May 1955 (all chapters and preview trailer) by Republic Pictures Corporation. VastVision. RCA Photophone recording. Chapter 1, 20 minutes; all other chapters, 13 minutes each.

    Chapter titles: 1–Daredevils of the Air. 2–Death Takes the Wheel. 3–The Trap That Failed. 4–Operation Murder. 5–The Mechanical Bloodhound. 6–Undersea Peril. 7–High Hazard. 8–Death Alley. 9–Cave of Doom. 10–The Masked Executioner. 11–Undersea Warfare. 12–Vengeance Under the Big Top.

    Cast: *Bert King* Harry Lauter, *June Edwards* Fran Bennett, *Daley* Keith Richards, *Jess Carter* Robert Shayne, *Zorn* Gregory Gay, *Art Kern* Rick Vallin, *Jim Hayes* Robert Clarke, *Travis* Terry Frost, *Sam* Mauritz Hugo, *Hank* Lee Roberts, *Bill* Chris Mitchell, *Mack* Stuart Whitman, *Matt Winston* Tom Steele, *Garth* George DeNormand, *Burton* Bill Scully, *Hal* Tom McDonough, *Mike* Harry Hollins, *Screaming woman* Jean Harvey, *Rigger* Bert LeBaron, *Rigger* Edwin Parker, *Tent worker* Brick Sullivan, *Tent worker* Richard Alexander, *Tent worker* Ray Spiker, *Watchman* Guy Teague, *Woman* Dorothy Andre, *Man* John Cason, *Man* Fenton "Duke" Taylor, *Man* Godfrey Wainwright.

Appendix

Republic's first official chapterplay was a sequel to a Mascot production, information about which follows for those who wish to compare the two serials.

The Lost Jungle
(22 March 1934)

Credits: *Producer* Nat Levine, *Directors* Armand Schaefer, David Howard, *Screenplay* Barney A. Sarecky, David Howard, Armand Schaefer, Wyndham Gittens, *Story* Colbert Clark, John Rathmell, Sherman Lowe, Al Martin, *Production supervisor* Victor Zobel, *Production manager* J. Laurence Wickland, *Business manager* Albert E. Levoy, *Cinematography* Alvin Wyckoff, William Nobles, *Supervising editor* Wyndham Gittens, *Editor* Earl Turner, *Musical score* Hal Chasnoff, *Sound* Terry Kellum, International Sound Recording Company, *Special effects* Howard Lydecker, Theodore Lydecker, *Wild animals and circus equipment* The Hagenbeck-Wallace Circus, *Optical effects* Consolidated Film Industries. A Nat Levine presentation. Copyright 22 March 1934 by Mascot Pictures Corporation. RCA Photophone recording. Chapter 1, 30 minutes; all other chapters, 18 minutes each.

Chapter titles: 1–Noah's Ark Island. 2–Nature in the Raw. 3–The Hypnotic Eye. 4–The Pit of Crocodiles. 5–Gorilla Warfare. 6–The Battle of Beasts. 7–The Tiger's Prey. 8–The Lion's Brood. 9–Eyes of the Jungle. 10–Human Hyenas. 11–The Gorilla. 12–Take Them Back Alive.

Also released on 22 March 1934 in a somewhat unusual chapterplay version consisting of a 73-minute feature, which contained chapters 1 and 2 plus approximately 24 minutes not in the regular serial, followed by the remaining chapters. A 106-minute feature version, *The Lost Jungle,* culled from the entire chapterplay was released on 13 June 1934.

Cast: *Clyde Beatty* Clyde Beatty, *Ruth Robinson* Cecilia Parker, *Larry Henderson* Syd Saylor, *Sharkey* Warner Richmond, *Kirby* Wheeler Oakman, *Thompson* Maston Williams, *Explorer* J. Crauford Kent, *Howard* Lloyd Whitlock, *Bannister* Lloyd Ingraham, *Captain Robinson* Edward J.

A poster for *The Lost Jungle* (1934).

LeSaint, *Flynn* Lew Meehan, *Slade* Max Wagner, *Jackman* Wes Warner, *Cook* Jack Carlyle, *Steve* Jim Corey, *Sandy* Wally Wales [Hal Taliaferro], *Pete* Ernest S. Adams, *Slim* Charles "Slim" Whitaker, *Maitland* Harry Holman, *Mickey* Mickey Rooney, *Man* George F. "Gabby" Hayes, *Man* Henry Hall, *Man* Lionel Backus, *Man* Wilfrid Lucas, *Killer lion* Sammie.

Index

135

M